08/09/19

CW00550989

Blessed Is She

Dreea,

I hope you enjoy the book.

I will miss you!

Love,

Pam G.

Blessed Is She

Lessons in Living from Women of the Bible

Elizabeth McDavid Jones

Copyright © 2014 by Elizabeth McDavid Jones

Cover design by Neil Alexander Heacox

ISBN: 978-1-4976-9394-4

Distributed by Open Road Distribution
345 Hudson Street
New York, NY 10014
www.openroadmedia.com

To Joanne Ullman Huggins, Elaine Carson, and Beth Everett
Their lives blessed many, especially me

Contents

Foreword

God is alive and well and speaks to His people today. He does this primarily through His living Word, the Bible. The goal for "Blessed is She" is to show today's women that God is speaking to *us*.

Blessed Is She is a book meant to lead women to the Bible, to be an aid in helping us understand how to read and study God's Word for ourselves, to apply it to our lives and to grow our faith. My hope is that, through this book, every woman may come to know that:

- the Bible is for her
- she can read the Bible and understand it
- the Bible is relevant and applicable to her life here and now
- the women in the Bible were women just like her, who experienced the same heartaches and spiritual trials she experiences
- the faith journey of every woman in the Bible is similar to her own

Regardless of our age, stage of life, or spiritual maturity, we have a lot to learn from the women of God we meet in Scripture. I sincerely hope this devotional Bible study will jumpstart you in your own discovery of Bible truths and life lessons, and even more important, the very heart of God for you. This study features a close-up look at Elizabeth, Mary the mother of Jesus, Mary of Bethany, Martha, and Naomi. Use the devotional pages for personal growth in your own quiet time with God and individual Bible reflection. To delve deeper, look up the verses for yourself to see what God's Word teaches about each Bible subject. But we also grow when we're in community, seeking to understand the Word of God together. So for group discussion or reflection, use the For Deeper Thought questions at the back of the book, or zoom into a more in-depth group focus with the 8-week "Elizabeth" Bible study.

My desire for this book is that every reader may come away with the sure knowledge that she is of great worth to God, and that God wants her to understand Who He is and what is His purpose for her life, through a deeper relationship with His Word.

Praying you'll be blessed,
Liz

Blessed Is She

"Blessed is she who believes that what the Lord has said to her will be accomplished."

Luke 1:45, NIV

Elizabeth

Day 1

First Things First

Bible Subject: Continuing; Faithfulness

Today's Reading: Luke 1:6-7

Today's Verse: "Both [Zechariah and Elizabeth] were upright in the sight of God, observing all the Lord's commandments and regulations blamelessly." Luke 1:6 (NIV)

Today's Lesson: *Elizabeth continued to do everything she knew God wanted her to do.*

Firsts are important in the lives of women: our first love, our first job, the birth of our first child. In the Bible, firsts are important, too. The first-born son received special privileges (Deut. 21:17). The Bible calls Jesus the "First and the Last" (Rev. 1:11). God raised Jesus from the dead on the first day of the week (John 20:1).

As we study the Bible, the first thing we're told about a person can give us insight into what the Holy Spirit wants to emphasize about that person. So what's the first thing we learn about Elizabeth? She and her husband were right with God. They knew the Word of God, and they lived it out in their lives.

But they still had no children.

Elizabeth was a godly woman—an *older,* godly woman. Spiritually, she'd done everything right. Yet the years had slipped by, and God had not blessed her with the desire of her heart—a baby.

Sometimes our lives are like Elizabeth's. We do everything we know God wants us to do. Yet the greatest desire of our heart eludes us: a husband, a baby, a career, a ministry. Year after year after year.

We can't help getting discouraged. We can't help wondering: *what am I doing wrong?* Why does God bless *everyone else* with what I want so much, but not me?

That's when we have to do what Elizabeth did: she just kept on doing what she knew was right. The Bible calls it *continuing.* 2 Timothy 3:14 says: "As for you, continue in what you have learned and become convinced of . . ."

When we continue in the Lord, doing what's right, even when we're discouraged, we're being obedient to God's Word. We're being faithful. And God always rewards faithfulness. *Always.*

Prayer: God, help me to continue being faithful to do what Your Word says, even when I feel discouraged.

[All Scripture quotations are in NIV unless otherwise noted]

Day 1

For more understanding:

To learn more about the importance of firsts in the Bible, you can read:

- that loving God is the *first* and greatest commandment (Mark 12:28-30)
- that in God's kingdom what we think is *first* may be last and the last *first* (Luke 13:30)
- that Jesus is the *first*-born of many spiritual brothers and sisters (Romans 8:29)

To learn more about continuing in the Lord, you can read:

- that *continuing* in the Word of God makes us true disciples (John 8:31)
- that we *continue* in Christ's love as we obey His instructions (John 15:10, Amplified)
- that we should *continue* in prayer (Colossians 4:2, KJV)

To learn more about how God rewards faithfulness, you can read:

- that God promises to bless *faithfulness* (Proverbs 28:20)
- that our *faithfulness* in small things results in God's trusting us with greater things (Matthew 25:21)
- that our *faithfulness* to Christ enables us to reign with Him in heaven (Rev. 17:14)

Day 2

God's Fringe Benefits

Bible Subject: Trusting God, God's Goodness

Today's Reading: Luke 1:5-7

Today's Verse: "But they had no children, because Elizabeth was barren, and they were both well along in years." Luke 1:7 (NIV)

Today's Lesson: *Elizabeth kept trusting in God's goodness.*

Growing older is harder than ever for women in today's beauty-oriented culture. As the ravages of time creep up on our physical bodies, a glance in the mirror can be a depressing experience. Our looks fade, our waistlines expand, our health and fitness decline. It's a rude awakening to realize that you're on the other side of middle-age.

But when it dawns on you that the greatest dream of your youth, that certain thing that you've hoped for all of your life, just isn't going to happen to you, *that* can be the bitterest pill of all to swallow.

This is what Elizabeth was facing. With every passing year, Elizabeth's dream of having a child seemed farther and farther out of reach.

Now she was old. Perhaps she was already past menopause. How her heart must have ached knowing that she'd never hold her own baby in her arms.

Yet Elizabeth never stopped trusting God. She kept believing in God's goodness to her, whether or not He granted her prayer for a child. Elizabeth knew that the benefits of serving God far outweighed that of any personal dream she had. She knew that only through God could the yearnings of her heart truly be satisfied.

As the wife of a priest, Elizabeth would have been familiar with Psalm 103:2-5: "Praise the Lord O my soul, and forget not all of His benefits . . . who satisfies your necessity and desire, at your personal age and situation, with good, so that your youth, renewed, is like the eagle's—strong, overcoming, soaring!" (Amplified Bible)

How encouraging are these words when we, at *any* age, find ourselves in difficult and seemingly hopeless circumstances. God satisfies us with good, no matter where we are in life. May we never forget the benefits of belonging to Him!

Prayer: Thank you, dear Lord, for your goodness and your many benefits. Help me to remember that You are my only hope and only you can truly satisfy.

Day 2

For more understanding:

To learn more about trusting God, you can read:

- that God provides richly for everything we need when we *trust* Him (1 Tim. 6:17)
- that *trusting* God keeps us from fear (Psalm 112:7)
- that *trusting* God makes us flourish like a tree planted by a stream (Jeremiah. 17:7-8)

To learn more about God's goodness and benefits to us, you can read:

- that God *benefits* us by carrying our burdens for us every day (Psalm 68:19)
- that God's *goodness* follows us wherever we go (Psalm 23:6)
- that we should rejoice in God's *goodness* (2 Chronicles 6:41)

To learn more about how God satisfies us, you can read:

- that God *satisfies* us with spiritual joy in great abundance (Jer 31:14)
- that God *satisfies* us with His presence (Psalm 65:4, KJV)
- that God *satisfies* the desires of every living thing (Psalm 145:16)

Day 3

Too Good to Believe

Bible Subject: Believing God's Word; Trusting God in Difficult Circumstances

Today's Reading: Luke 1:8-25

Today's Verses: "The angel answered [Zechariah], '. . . you will be silent and not be able to speak until the day this happens, because you did not believe my words.'" (Luke 1:19-20)

"'The Lord has done this for me,' [Elizabeth] said." (Luke 1:25a)

Today's Lesson: *Elizabeth trusted God enough to believe His promises to her.*

"If it sounds too good to be true, it probably isn't." This old adage could have come right out of the mouth of any parent trying to wise up a too-gullible child. We strive to teach our children that you can't trust just *anyone's* word. You have to *know* the person to know whether their word is trustworthy.

Yet Zechariah, a priest who had spent his life studying God's Word, didn't believe it when Gabriel told him "your prayer has been heard. Your wife Elizabeth will bear you a son . . ." (v. 12). Zechariah *knew* God. He should have believed the promise God was making to him. But he didn't.

Why?

Maybe it was because Zechariah thought that it was just too good to be happening to him. After years of praying for something that never came to pass, perhaps Zechariah had given up hope that it ever would. He had kept on praying out of habit, but somewhere along the way, he had stopped believing that God would answer. Zechariah had stopped trusting the reliability of God's Word.

But Elizabeth *hadn't* stopped trusting what God said. As soon as she found out that she was pregnant, she acknowledged God and rejoiced in His goodness to her.

When we endure periods of difficult circumstances, when our prayers go unanswered for weeks, months, or years, we may have trouble believing that anything good will ever happen to us again. But our response must be like Elizabeth's—to trust in the reliability of the promises God gives us in His Word. The Bible says, "For no matter how many promises God has made, they are Yes in Christ" (2 Cor. 1:20).

Because we know that God Himself is trustworthy, we know that we can believe the wonderful promises in His Word, even when it seems "too good to be true."

Prayer: Heavenly Father, I know Your Word is true and trustworthy. Help me in the tough times to continue holding fast to Your promises.

Day 3

For more understanding:

To learn more about the trustworthiness of God, you can read:

- that God is *trustworthy* because He can only speak the truth (Isaiah 45:19)
- that Jesus is *trustworthy* because He *is* the Truth (John 14:6)
- that the Holy Spirit is *trustworthy* because He is the Spirit of Truth (John 15:26)

To learn more about why we can believe God's Word, you can read:

- that *God's Word* is flawless (2 Sam. 22:31; Psalm 18:30)
- that Jesus is the Living *Word of God* (John 1:14)
- that *God's words* are true and trustworthy (Psalm 119:138; Rev. 22:6)

To learn more about God's promises to us, you can read:

- that His *promises* never fail (1 Kings 8:56)
- that God always remembers His *promises* (Psalm 105:42)
- that God's *promises* to us are great and precious (2 Peter 1:4)

Day 4

Fox-Hole Christians

Bible Subject: God's Presence; Acknowledging God

Today's Reading: Luke 1:8-25

Today's Verse: "The Lord has done this for me . . . In these days He has shown His favor and taken away my disgrace among the people." (Luke 1:25)

Today's Lesson: *Elizabeth acknowledged God and nurtured her relationship with Him in good times as well as hard times.*

In World War II, U.S. soldiers adopted a type of trench warfare called foxholes. These bottle-shaped, open holes in the ground shielded soldiers from artillery explosions and enemy bullets as they crouched inside and fired their weapons.* Often foxholes were the only thing that enabled soldiers to survive the battle.

Sometimes we can be foxhole *Christians.*

When we're "under fire" in our lives, we're quick to turn to God to get us through. But when things are going well again, we just as quickly forget Him. Maybe not *forget* Him really, just nudge Him aside, little by little, day by day, until the only time we think about Him is Sunday morning between 11 and 12. "My people have forgotten me days without number," God said through the prophet Jeremiah (Jeremiah 2:32).

Yet Elizabeth, in the joy of her long-awaited pregnancy, *didn't* forget God. Instead, she acknowledged God and praised Him for what He had done for her.

Then she did something very important. She went into seclusion. Why? Since we know that God intends everything in the Bible to teach us something (1 Cor. 10:6; 2 Tim. 3:16), we know we're meant to learn from Elizabeth's example. What are we supposed to learn here?

I believe it is this: When her prayer had been answered, in the midst of her immense happiness, Elizabeth set aside time in her life to experience God and grow in her relationship with Him. Elizabeth knew that her need for God was as great in times of joy and answered prayer as it was in times of trial.

So is ours. In all the times of our lives it is God's presence that sustains us. We must never be so busy—or so happy—that we neglect our relationship with Him.

Prayer: Dear God, I don't want to be a foxhole Christian I don't want to only turn to You when I'm in trouble. Help me to spend time with You daily. Thank you for being here for me.

*Wikipedia, "Defensive Fighting Positions"

Day 4

For more understanding:

To learn more about why we need to come into God's presence, you can read:

- that only in *God's presence* is there fullness of joy (Psalm 16:11)
- that God receives glory and honor when we come into *His presence* (1 Chron. 16:27)
- that the *presence of the Lord* sustains us and saves us (Psalm 51:11-12)

To learn more about how the Bible teaches us, you can read:

- that every incident in the Bible *teaches* by presenting a spiritual example (1 Cor. 10:6)
- that every word in the Bible is useful for *teaching* us how we should live (2 Tim. 3:16)
- that, through the Bible, God *teaches* us what is best for us (Isaiah 48:17)

To learn more about why we should acknowledge God always, you can read:

- that, when we *acknowledge* God before other people, Jesus acknowledges us before His Father (Matthew 10:32)
- that *acknowledging* Jesus before others shows that we belong to Him (1 John 4:3)
- that God intends for every living creature to praise and *acknowledge* Him
- (Psalm 145:21)

Day 5

In the Name of God

Bible Subject: The Character of God, Trusting in God's Name

Today's Reading: Luke 1:23-25

Today's Verse: "In these days He has shown His favor and taken away my disgrace among the people." (Luke 1:25)

Today's Lesson: *Elizabeth knew God's character and trusted in His reputation.*

One of the first things we teach our children about the Bible is the importance of the Ten Commandments. Mostly a list of do's and don'ts, it's straightforward stuff—and easy to understand. But here's one that's more elusive: You shall not take the Lord's name in vain. Or, as the NIV Bible translates: "You shall not misuse the name of the Lord your God, for the Lord will not hold anyone guiltless who misuses His Name"(Deut. 5:11).

That sounds serious. Why is God's name so important?

Because His name represents Who He is—His character. We use

the expression "my good name" to mean our *reputation*. So, misusing *God's* name is the same as attacking *His* reputation. Likewise, trusting in God's name means you're putting your trust in Who God is. The Bible tells us that Jesus came so that people everywhere would put their hope in His name (Matthew 12:21).

Elizabeth knew God's character. She'd spent time learning about Him and experiencing Him through prayer. She knew His Word well (Luke 1:6). She recognized "the wonder of God's great love" (Psalm 17:7). She realized God heard her prayers and would respond with encouragement (Psalm 10:17). She understood that God would be faithful to keep His promise to "bless the righteous [and] surround them with favor as with a shield" (Psalm 3:12).

Because she knew God's reputation, Elizabeth could confidently put her trust in His name. "Some trust in chariots and horses," the Bible says in Psalm 20:7, "but we trust in the Name of the Lord our God."

We too can trust in God's reputation. The more time we spend getting to know God and experiencing Him for ourselves, the more boldly we can say, "My ears had *heard* of You, but now my eyes have *seen* You!" (Job 42:5).

Prayer: Dear God, give me more understanding about Your great name.

Day 5

For more understanding:

To learn more about how God's Character is represented by His Name, you can read:

- that *God's Name* is holy (Luke 1:49)
- that *God's Name* is majestic (Psalm 8:1)
- that *Jesus' Name* is called Wonderful, Counselor, Mighty God, Everlasting Father, and Prince of Peace (Isaiah 9:6, KJV)

To learn more about trusting in God's reputation by trusting in His Name, you can read:

- that God saves us because of *His Name's* sake (Psalm 106:8)
- that our sins are forgiven on account of *His Name* (1 John 2:12)
- that God guides us along the right paths for *His Name's* sake (Psalm 23:3)

To learn more about what happens when we believe in God's Name, you can read:

- that believing in *God's Name* gives us the right to become His children (John 1:12)
- that we receive salvation when we call upon *His Name* (Romans 10:13, Joel 2:32)
- that we please God when we believe in *His Name* (1 John 3:23)

Day 6

Confidence in Confidence

Bible Subject: Confidence in God; Surrendering our Lives to God's Control

Today's Reading: Luke 1:39-45

Today's Verse: ". . . the baby leaped in her womb, and Elizabeth was filled with and controlled by the Holy Spirit . . . In a loud voice she exclaimed, 'How have I deserved that the honor should be granted to me that the mother of my Lord should come to me?'" (Luke 1:41b-43, Amplified and NIV)

Today's Lesson: *Elizabeth had confidence in God and gave control of her life to Him.*

We live in a culture that proclaims self-confidence as the gateway to success in almost every area of our lives, especially for women. Everything our culture values in women is linked to self-confidence. If we only believe in ourselves, we'll be independent, beautiful, popular, and deliriously happy. Self-confidence will get us a job, a husband, and maybe even make us rich. "I have confidence in confidence alone," sings Maria in the *Sound of Music*. "I have confidence in me!" Translated: If only we have confidence in ourselves, we can accomplish anything!

An inspiring message, for sure. But not one that we can count on.

Self-confidence can fail us, but God never can. The Bible tells us we're not to trust in ourselves (Philippians 3:3). Instead we're to put our confidence in God (Psalm 118:8). Putting confidence in God means we submit ourselves to the influence of His Spirit rather than the influence of the world (James 4:4-7). It means we give control of our lives to God because we trust Him completely. "The Lord will be your confidence," says Proverbs 3:26. "He will keep your foot from being snared."

Elizabeth did this. We learn in Luke 1:41 (Amplified Version) that Elizabeth was "filled with and controlled by the Holy Spirit." Because she surrendered control of her will to God, God used her to pronounce the very first prophecy about Who Jesus was! When she put her confidence in God, she could boldly, "in a loud voice," speak out what the Holy Spirit impressed upon her heart. "Confidence [in God] shall be your strength," says Isaiah 30:15 (Amplified Version).

When we count on God rather than ourselves, we never come up short!

Prayer: Dear God, cause me to put my confidence in You each and every day. Teach me to surrender control of my life to Your loving care and to rest in the confidence in Your love.

Day 6

For more understanding:

To learn more about confidence in God, you can read:

- that people everywhere can put their *confidence* in God's righteous deeds (Psalm 65:5)
- how we can approach God with *confidence* through our relationship with Jesus (Ephesians 3:12, Hebrews 4:16)
- that when we put our *confidence* in Jesus, we're able to live for God's glory instead of our own (Ephesians 1:12)

To learn more about submitting our lives to God's control, you can read:

- that *submission* to God's Spirit brings life and peace (Hebrews 12:9)
- that God's unfailing love surrounds us when we *submit* our lives to His control (Psalm 32:9-10)
- that *submitting* our lives to God's Spirit sets our minds on what He desires (Romans 8:5)

To learn more about how the Holy Spirit speaks to us in our hearts, you can read:

- that the Holy Spirit reveals the truth about Jesus to our *hearts* (John 15:16)
- how the Holy Spirit enlightens the eyes of our *heart* with wisdom and revelation (Ephesians 1:17-18)
- that the Holy Spirit impresses upon our *hearts* how we should pray (Romans 8:27)

Day 7

The Gift That Keeps on Giving

Bible Subject: The Gifts of the Holy Spirit

Today's Reading: Luke 1:24-25, 39-45

Today's Verse: "When Elizabeth heard Mary's greeting, [her] baby leaped in her womb, and Elizabeth was filled with the Holy Spirit." (Luke 1:41)

Today's Lesson: *Elizabeth opened her heart to God's Spirit and received the spiritual gifts He had for her.*

Women love gifts, both giving and receiving them. Not so much because of what the gifts *are* but because of what they *mean*. Gifts send a message of love and caring to the important people in our lives. Few things bring more joy than seeing the eyes of that special person light up when we hand them a carefully-selected present wrapped up in a big, bright bow.

God loves to give gifts to us, too. Jesus is our greatest gift from God (John 4:10), but the Holy Spirit is another good gift God has for us (Luke 11:13). What's more, through the Holy Spirit, God gives us more of Himself, bestowing wonderful spiritual gifts upon us that help us know Him better, equip us to live the Christian life more effectively, and enable us to build up the church by encouraging and ministering to others (John 14:26, Romans 12:6-8).

One of the spiritual gifts God gave Elizabeth was discernment. Through the power of the Holy Spirit, Elizabeth was able to tell the difference between a normal movement of the baby in her womb and the baby's leap of joy to be in the presence of Mary, who was pregnant with Jesus. Such revelation or wisdom from God is called discernment (Luke 12:56, 1 Cor. 2:14, Hebrews 5:14).

God wants us to eagerly desire every spiritual gift He's chosen for us (1 Cor. 12:31, 14:1). Just as carefully as we select the right gift for *our* loved ones, God, because He loves us so much, decides upon the right spiritual gifts for *us*!

Prayer: Lord, fill me today with Your Spirit. I greatly desire every gift that You have for me. Give me insight to recognize the gifts You choose for me, and show me how to use them in accordance with Your will and for the fulfillment of Your purposes.

Day 7

For more understanding:

To learn more about how God chooses spiritual gifts for us, you can read:
- that each person has his or her own *gift* from God (1 Cor. 7:7, 1 Peter 4:10)
- that God determines each person's spiritual *gifts* (1 Cor. 12:11)
- that God distributes *gifts* of the Holy Spirit according to His Will and by the unmerited favor He gives us through His grace (Heb. 2:4, 1 Peter 4:10)

To learn more about the gifts of the Holy Spirit, you can read:
- that the greatest *gift* is love (1 Cor. 13:1-13)
- that spiritual *gifts* vary greatly, from artistic ability to prophetic dreams and visions to leadership and showing mercy (Exodus 31:3, Acts 2:4, 17-18, Romans 12:6-8)
- that spiritual *gifts* are given to us for God's purposes and are to be used according to His Will (Exodus 31:4, Colossians 1:9, 1 Cor. 14:12)

To learn more about how God desires us to use our spiritual gifts, you can read:
- that we are to use our *spiritual gifts* to benefit each other (1 Peter 4:10) and to build up the church (1 Cor. 14:12)
- how *spiritual gifts* help us praise God and give Him thanks (Ephesians 5:18b-20)
- that our *spiritual gifts* are meant to help us make known the salvation of God (Hebrews 2:3-4)

Day 8

God's Secret Ingredient

Bible Subject: Faith in God's Word

Today's Reading: Luke 1:5-17, 39-45, 57-66

Today's Verse: "Blessed is she who believes that what the Lord has said to her will be accomplished." (Luke 1:45)

Today's Lesson: *Elizabeth made God's Word the source of her faith.*

Every good cook has a secret ingredient that she uses in her special dishes. Whether it's a pinch of saffron in rice or cayenne chili in chocolate sauce, the secret ingredient gives the dish its power to please whoever tastes it.

There's a "secret" ingredient that powers our faith lives, too—the Word of God. God spoke through Moses that we're to live by every word that comes from His mouth (Deut. 8:3). In Luke 1:6, we read that Elizabeth "observed all the Lord's commandments . . . blamelessly." This doesn't mean that she never sinned, only that God counted her faith in His Word as righteousness (Genesis 15:6; Romans 4:2-5, 23-25).

Elizabeth had great faith, and it was God's Word that powered her faith—and her life. She believed that what God said was true, and she acted on that faith. When relatives pressured her to name her baby after her husband, she insisted instead on the name *John*, the name that God had chosen and revealed to her husband through the angel Gabriel. Elizabeth didn't have to *see* the angel herself in order to believe the Word from God that the angel had spoken. The Bible says that we're supposed to live by faith, not by sight (2 Cor. 5:7). The source of Elizabeth's faith was her belief in the truth of God's Word.

Like Elizabeth, we must look to God's Word to be the source of *our* faith. "Faith comes by hearing," Romans 10:17 says, "and hearing by the word of God."

God's Word is our best recipe for faith. When we take God at His Word, believing in the truth of what He speaks to us though the Bible and in our hearts, God uses our faith to work out His purposes in our lives (Romans 8:28). And unlike our own concoctions in the kitchen, nothing God does ever turns out wrong!

Prayer: Lord, cause me to trust in the truth of Your Word, and teach me to live by faith in Your Word.

Day 8

For more understanding:

To learn more about why faith in God's Word is so important, you can read:

- that *God's Word* and God Himself are inseparable (John 1:1)
- that Jesus is the *Word of God* made flesh (John 1:14)
- that the *Word of Christ* dwells in us and empowers us for ministry (Colossians 3:16)

To learn more about the truth of God's Word, you can read:

- that the *truth* of God's Word is everlasting (Psalm 119:152)
- that God's Word is itself *Truth* and by it we are consecrated to Him (John 17:17)
- that the Word of *truth* is the gospel of our salvation (Ephesians 1:13)

To learn more about what happens when we let faith in God's Word power our lives, you can read:

- that our love for God is perfected when we *let God's Word direct our lives* (1 John 2:5, Amplified)
- that *acting on God's Word*, rather than just listening to it, brings spiritual blessing (James 1:22-25)
- that God's Word becomes our greatest joy when we *consume it and make it a part of our lives* (Jeremiah 15:16)

Mary

Day 9

If You Say So

Bible Subject: Believing the Impossible; God's Omnipotence

Today's Reading: Genesis 18:1-15, 21:1-5; Luke 1:26-38

Today's Verse: "Nothing is impossible with God." (Luke 1:37)

Today's Lesson: *Mary believed God could do the impossible in her life.*

Two women, Sarah and Mary. One very old, the other very young. Both received a promise from God—the birth of a son. Trouble is, for both women, that birth was impossible.

Sarah was 90 years old, well past menopause. She had long since given up on having a child of her own. Mary, on the other hand, was barely into puberty, and she was a virgin. Both women knew the facts of life. Post-menopausal women and virgins *don't* have babies. Yet Sarah and Mary both received a Word from God that He intended to accomplish the impossible in her life.

How did each woman respond to God's wonderful—but impossible promise?

33

Mary instantly put aside her human understanding and took God at His Word. "May it be to me as you have said," Mary replied (Luke 1:38). And Sarah? Well, Sarah laughed. "After I am worn out and my husband is old, will I now have this pleasure?" she thought (Genesis 18:12).

Nope, ain't gonna happen, was Sarah's response.

Lord, if you say so, I believe, was Mary's.

The Bible tells us that nothing is too hard for the Lord (Genesis 18:14). God is in the business of doing impossible things, and He wants to do them in our lives too—if only we believe. "Everything is possible for those who believe," Jesus says in Mark 9:23. *Everything.* The one requirement God has is our faith. We must believe that God is *able* to do great things in our lives (Romans 4:21), and that He *wants* to do them (Mark 11:24), just as He promises us in His Word.

That's it. God's requirement for doing the impossible. It was the same for Sarah and Mary *then* as it is for us *now*. Believe that He can—and that He wants to.

What will our response be to Him today?

Prayer: Lord, help me, like Mary, to accept You at Your Word. Help me to trust You for the impossible in my life.

Day 9

For more understanding:

To learn more about God's power to do whatever He wants to do (omnipotence), you can read:

- that God's great *power* working in and for us who believe is immeasurable, unlimited and unsurpassed by any other (Ephesians 1:19, Amplified)
- that God has the *power* to fulfill His every purpose and every act prompted by our faith in Him (2 Thessalonians 1:11, NIV and Amplified)
- that God's *power* is exalted and so great that it is beyond our understanding (Job 37:23, NIV and Amplified)

To learn more about God's desire to do good things for us, you can read:

- that it was God's *desire* that His perfect Son would bear our sins through the sacrifice of His life, so that we could be made right with God (Isaiah 53:10-12)
- that it is God's pleasure and *desire* to adopt us as His children through Jesus Christ (Ephesians 1:5)
- that God *wants* to give us the desires of our heart, if only we delight ourselves in Him (Psalm 37:4)

To learn more about believing God for the impossible, you can read:

- that God performed the *impossible* when He raised Jesus from the dead (Acts 2:24)
- that nothing is *impossible* for those who firmly trust in the Lord (Matthew 17:20, Amplified)
- that what is humanly *impossible* is possible for God (Luke 18:27)

Day 10

I Get It Now!

Bible Subject: A Response of Faith, Spiritual Understanding

Today's Reading: Luke 1:26-38

Today's Verse: "How will this be, since I am a virgin?" (Luke 1:34)

Today's Lesson: *Mary asked God for the understanding she needed to respond to His Word in faith.*

Not how can this be, but how will it be? The word *can* asks the question is this possible? The word *will* only wonders how.

Mary was a virgin when the angel Gabriel appeared to her and told her that God intended to do the impossible in her life: that she would become pregnant with God's own Son. Mary didn't question whether God was able to do what He said. Neither did she question whether it was *really* God's desire to bless her in such an awe-inspiring way. We know nothing of Mary before she had this encounter with an angel. But we can be sure of one thing: Mary had to have had an amazing relationship with God. She obviously knew Him well, and trusted Him totally. How else could she have accepted without question the mind-blowing promise God was making to her through Gabriel?

Mary responded with faith to God's Word, believing that God could accomplish in her life whatever purpose, or calling, He had for her (Romans 8:28).

Yet faith doesn't mean never wanting to know the *how*. God has given us minds to think and understand, and wondering *how* something will happen is not a lack of faith. In fact, God *promises* in the Bible that He *will* give us understanding if we ask him in faith (James 1:5).

God may not always reveal to us exactly how something will happen, as He did with Mary, but He will *always* give us more understanding or wisdom than we would have had if we didn't ask Him for it at all. Just as He did with Mary, God gives *us* the right measure of understanding at the right time to be able to walk in faith in our particular situation. In that way, we can continue to trust Him for each *new* situation, and our faith can grow.

Prayer: Lord, You are so good to give me wisdom and understanding when I ask. Help me to say "Yes, Lord" to whatever You ask me to do.

Day 10

For more understanding:

To learn more about responding with faith to God's Word, you can read:

- that God strengthens our faith when we *firmly put our trust in His promises* (Romans 4:20)
- that God teaches us to rely on Him when we *put our hope in His Word* (Psalm 130:5-6)
- that God is our refuge and shield when we *put our hope in His Word* (Psalm 119:114)

To learn more about the purpose or calling God has for each of our lives, you can read:

- that each of us is chosen by God for a *purpose* according to His plan (Ephesians 1:11)
- that we are called to live holy lives because of God's *purpose* for us (2 Timothy 1:9; 1 Thess. 4:7)
- that we all have a *calling* or ministry to reflect God's glory through the way we live our lives (2 Corinthians 3:18-4:1, Amplified)

To learn more about seeking understanding or wisdom from God, you can read:

- that we can pray for *wisdom and understanding* and God will give it to us through His Spirit (Ephesians 1:17-19)
- that God grants *understanding* to us when we call out to Him for it (Proverbs 2:3-6)
- that we gain *understanding* from God's Word (Psalm 119:100, 104)

Day 11

You've Got to be Kidding

Bible Subject: Having a Right Heart before God

Today's Reading: Luke 1:26-38

Today's Verse: "Hail, O favored one! The Lord is with you! Favored by God are you before all other women!" (Luke 1:28, Amplified)

Today's Lesson: *Mary had a humble, worshipful, and willing heart.*

Favored above all women? *Really?* A teenage girl in a dusty village in the middle of nowhere, from one of the poorest families in town? God, you're kidding, right? You sent your angel to *her?*

Doesn't seem to make much sense, does it? It didn't to Mary either. The Bible tells us how she felt: "greatly troubled and disturbed and confused at what he said and kept revolving in her mind what such a greeting might mean" (v. 29, Amplified).

Mary's reaction to the angel's words is our best clue to the reason that she *was* so favored by God: she didn't have the slightest idea why anyone would say such a thing to *her.*

Mary had an attitude of heart that God loves: humble, worshipful, and willing. The Bible often calls this a "right" or a "pure" heart, or a "right" spirit, as in Psalm 51:10 (KJV). The right attitude of heart was one requirement God always had in the job description for every man or woman in the Bible whom He used in a great way. Mary had it. So did Abraham, David, Moses, Ruth, Hannah, Elizabeth and many, many more.

Time and again in the Bible, God makes it clear that it's our heart that He most cares about. "The Lord does not look at the things man looks at," says 1 Samuel 16:7. "Man looks at the outward appearance, but the Lord looks at the heart."

What does this mean?

It means when God looked at Mary, He didn't see a confused and frightened teenage girl. He saw a young woman who loved Him with all her heart, and who was willing to make herself available to Him to be used however He saw fit.

The right heart condition was all God required of Mary. And it's all He requires of us.

Prayer: Lord, I want a right heart. Make my heart humble, willing, and always worshipful toward You.

Day 11

For more understanding:

To learn more about what is a right heart towards God, you can read:

- that the Lord is close to the *broken-hearted* and those whose *spirits are humble* (Psalm 34:18)
- that Jesus called Himself *gentle and humble in heart* (Matthew 11:29)
- that God loves the inner beauty of *a gentle and peaceful spirit* (1 Peter 3:4)

To learn more about how God "looks" at our hearts, you can read:

- that God *searches our hearts* and knows everything we think and feel (Psalm 139:23)
- that God's Word *judges the thoughts and attitudes of our hearts* and nothing is hidden from Him (Hebrews 4:12)
- that God knows us and understands us and *knows the extent of our devotion to Him* (Jeremiah 12:3 Amplified)

To learn more about why God cares so much about the condition of our hearts, you can read:

- that *a pure heart* enables us to "see" God, or fully experience Him (Matthew 5:8)
- that being able to come into God's presence requires *a heart that is right before Him* (Psalm 24:3-6)
- that our words and actions, for good or bad, are *a reflection for what is in our hearts* (Matthew 12:45, Mark 7:21, Luke 6:45)

Day 12

At Your Service, God

Bible Subject: A Submissive Spirit; Brokenness of Spirit; A Servant's Heart

Today's Reading: Luke 1:26-38

Today's Verses: "I am the Lord's servant . . . May it be to me as you have said." (Luke 1:38)

"The sacrifice acceptable to God is a broken spirit: a broken and contrite heart; such O God, you will not despise" Psalm 51:17 (Amplified)

Today's Lesson: *Mary submitted her will to God's leadership so that she could serve Him in whatever way He wanted to use her.*

In the old American West, wild horses were rounded up and "broken," so that they could be used for riding, cattle-herding, or other chores. Breaking a horse meant to bring its will into the submission of its rider, so that the horse would accept human leadership. A horse that couldn't be broken couldn't be useful on the ranch.

Biblical broken-ness has a similar meaning. To have "a broken and contrite heart" (Psalm 51:17) means that our spirit is submitted to God. It means that we're "at God's service," that we're willing—and eager—to accept His leadership in our lives. "You are my Rock and my Fortress," says David in Psalm 31:3, "therefore . . . lead me and guide me." When Mary said that she was "the Lord's servant," she was showing that she had a heart eager to be useful to God, a heart that was "broken" to do God's will rather than her own.

Remember the saying, "If it ain't broke, don't fix it"? God values our broken-ness of spirit because a heart submitted to Him is one that He can "fix" and make better than it was before. The Bible tells us that if our hearts "ain't broke," God can't fix them

(Ezekiel 11:19, 2 Corinthians 3:3) Not that He isn't *able* to. God wants to give us a choice. We're not like wild horses, forced into being broken. God wants us to *choose* His leadership in our lives, not be forced into it. Unless we choose spiritual broken-ness, we *will* be like an unbroken horse—not much use to God for doing His Work.

Mary didn't have to be coerced into cooperating with God's plans. As soon as God revealed His purpose for her, she put herself at His complete disposal. Mary's answer to God's calling on her life was, Here I am, Lord. Use me however You desire.

May it also be ours.

Prayer: Lord, give me a submissive heart—a servant's heart—that I would freely choose to serve You.

Day 12

For more understanding:

To learn more about how God "fixes" us back better than we were before, when we come to him in a spirit of broken-ness, you can read:

- that Jesus came to bind up and heal *the broken-hearted*, and bring us into right standing with God (Luke 4:18; Isaiah 61:1-3, Amplified)
- that God guides and comforts us, revives our spirits, and gives us hearts of praise instead of sadness, when we have *a contrite heart* (Isaiah 57:15, 18)
- that God is near to us when we have *a broken heart*, and He redeems our lives and gives us a Refuge in Him (Psalm 34:18, 22)

To learn more about having the heart of a servant, you can read:

- that Jesus came not to be served, but *to serve others*, and to exchange His life as a ransom for ours (Matthew 20:25-28)
- that whoever wants to be greatest in God's eyes must have *an attitude of servant-hood* toward everyone else (Mark 10:43-44)
- that we're supposed to model in our own lives Christ's *attitude of servant-hood* (John 13:13-17)

To learn more about how God uses us when we have willing hearts of service to Him, you can read:

- that, when we're *willing* and obedient to God, he uses us to bring justice to the oppressed and encourage and help people in need (Isaiah 1:17, 19)
- that God uses us to minister to others when our hearts are *willing* and eagerly to serve Him (2 Peter 5:2-3)
- that God uses our natural talents and skills for His Work when we *willingly* make ourselves available to Him for His Purposes (1 Chronicles 29:1-5)

Day 13

It's Time!

Bible Subject: God's Timing; Sensitivity to the Holy Spirit

Today's Reading: Luke 1:39-44, 56, 67-79

Today's Verse: "At that time, Mary got ready and hurried to a town in the hill country of Judea, where she entered Zechariah's home and greeted Elizabeth." (Luke 1:39-40)

Today's Lesson: *Mary cooperated with God's perfect timing for His purposes by obeying the urging of the Holy Spirit.*

We live in a world where time matters. Time runs our lives. We have clocks, phones, and IPODs that remind us what time it is. Yet this sort of "time" is something we've invented—it doesn't really exist. It's only a measurement we use to describe the turning of the earth on its axis.

But "God's timing" is something that is real. The Bible tells us in Ecclesiastes 3:1-8 (KJV), "To everything there is a season, and a time to every purpose under heaven." God's timing means that there is an exact right time for every purpose of God to unfold.

We see this at work in Mary's story.

After Gabriel delivered his message to Mary, Mary immediately "got ready and hurried" to her cousin Elizabeth's house. Why? Perhaps God was urging Mary to do something that couldn't wait, something that could only be done at Zechariah and Elizabeth's house. What was it?

Could it have been that Mary needed to learn everything God's Word said about the Son she was to bear? As a girl from a poor family, Mary would not have had the opportunity to go to school to study God's Word, as the village boys would have done.

Yet in the house of Zechariah, Mary could learn from an expert. Zechariah, a priest, knew the Word of God well. What's more, since Mary stayed there 3 months (v. 56), she would have been present when Elizabeth's baby was born and would have heard Zechariah's prophecy (vv. 67-79) about Mary's own Son, Jesus.

God designed the perfect preparation for Mary to mother His Son. But Mary had to cooperate with God's timing by listening to the urging of His Spirit in her heart—and acting on it.

We too need to be sensitive to the Holy Spirit's urging. We don't want to miss God's perfect timing for the purposes He has for us!

Prayer: Lord God, I don't want to miss anything You want to do in my life. Help me to hear Your voice and obey.

Day 13

For more understanding:

To learn more about God's perfect timing, you can read:

- that Jesus knew there was an *exact right time* determined by God for Him to begin His ministry (John 2:4), for His betrayal (Matt. 26:45), for His death and Resurrection (John 17:1), and for His Second Coming (Mark 13:32)
- that God by His own authority has set *a time and date* for every occurrence (Acts 1:7)
- how God promises that at the *proper time* we will see and experience the advantages to us and others of all that we do for Him (Galatians 6:9-10 Amplified)

To learn more about God's purposes, you can read:

- how God's *purposes* stand firm, and everything He plans, He accomplishes (Isaiah 46:10b, 11b)
- that God works out everything for good in the life of each believer according to His *purpose* (Romans 8:28)
- that, no matter what, God's *purposes* always prevail (Proverbs 19:21)

To learn more about being sensitive to the Holy Spirit, you can read:

- that when we're sensitive to Him, the *Holy Spirit* can teach us and remind us of the Word of God (John 14:26)
- that the *Holy Spirit* helps us know how to pray, if we are sensitive to His voice (Romans 8:26-27)
- that being sensitive to the *Holy Spirit* can help us understand the things of God (1 Cor. 2:12)

Day 14

I Give Up!

Bible Subject: Obedience to God's Will; Listening to God

Today's Reading: Luke 1:26-38: Genesis 16:1-16

Today's Verse: "Behold the handmaid of the Lord: be it unto me according to Thy Word."(Luke 1:38, KJV)

Today's Lesson: *Mary chose to listen to God's voice and do His will instead of her own.*

In the Bible, the word *handmaid* often means *bondservant,* or slave.*
Hagar was the handmaiden of Sarai, Abram's wife. As a slave, Hagar
didn't have the option of doing her own will; she had to obey the will
of her mistress. When Sarai ordered Hagar to sleep with Abram, Hagar
didn't have a choice in the matter. And when Hagar became pregnant
with Abram's child, Hagar didn't have the right to claim the baby as her
own. Even Hagar's son belonged to Sarai!

Mary's statement that she was the "handmaid of the Lord" meant
that she was relinquishing all her rights to do as she chose. Instead of

her own will, she would do God's will. Mary showed her willing heart by *choosing* to obey God.

Obedience would be supremely important for Mary. She would have the job of mothering the Son of God. As Jesus grew up, Mary would need to be an example to Him of unwavering and exact obedience to the Lord. Our God is a God of perfection. His Son had to be reared perfectly. Who could be trusted with such a vital task? No one on earth; we're not capable of perfection. No, only God Himself could do the job. So God chose someone—Mary—whose heart was in complete submission to His Will.

God knew that Mary's submissive heart meant that she would listen to His voice and obey it without question, exactly as He told her to. Through Mary's obedience, God Himself could rear Jesus!

God can do great things through us, too—if we let Him. He has a standard for us to follow as well: His Word. Alone, we're not capable of obeying God's standards. We, like Mary, must allow God Himself to do the job—through our submissive hearts.

Prayer: Lord, work obedience in my heart. Through the power of Your Spirit, teach me to obey You exactly as You say in Your Word. Help me to desire to do Your will, not mine.

Harper's Bible Dictionary, p. 929

Day 14

For more understanding:

To learn more about willing obedience to God, you can read:

- that our *faithful obedience* to God comes from our love for Him (Deut. 11:13)
- that when we are *willing in our hearts to be obedient* to God's standards, He sets us free from being slaves to sin and brings us into complete conformity with His Will (Romans 6:17-18, Amplified)
- that every believer is called through the Holy Spirit to *a willing obedience* to Christ (1 Peter 1:2, Amplified)

To learn more about listening to God's voice, you can read:

- that we receive a blessing when we *hear the Word of God* and obey it (Luke 11:28)
- that God has more delight in our obedience to *His Voice* than He does in any offering or sacrifice we may make (1 Sam. 15:22, Amplified)
- that those who know Jesus know *His Voice* and allow themselves to be led by it (John 10:27)

To learn more about how we can't live up to God's standards on our own, you can read:

- that unless we put our faith in God it is impossible for us to please Him or *satisfy His standards* (Hebrews 11:6 Amplified)
- that we can only be made right with God through the righteousness of Christ, since there is no one who could ever be good enough to *live up to God's standards* (Romans 3:12, 23-24)
- that without God's help no one alive could be considered righteous according to *His standards* (Psalm 143:2)

Day 15

Give It All You've Got

Bible Subject: Right Worship

Today's Reading: Luke 1:46-56

Today's Verse: "And Mary said, 'My soul magnifies and extols the Lord . . . and my spirit rejoices in God my Savior.'" (Luke 1:46-47, Amplified)

Today's Lesson: *Mary worshipped God with her whole being.*

The best chefs often craft their menus around the availability of fresh local ingredients. They know that what you put into a dish dramatically affects the end result.

Worshipping the Lord works the same way. What we put into worship also affects the end result. Jesus says there is a right way and a wrong way to worship God (John 4:23-24). We're supposed to worship in spirit and in "truth." The Amplified Bible translates "truth" in these verses as "reality" and "true worshipers" as "genuine worshipers."

Real worship. *Genuine* worship. What is it? And how do we do it?

How do we find the right ingredients to put into our worship so that we will be "the kind of worshippers the Father seeks" (John 4:23b)?

Mary knew. We see in her song (Luke 1:46-47) the ingredients Mary put into her worship: her whole being—body, soul, and spirit. The Bible says she magnified and extolled Him in her soul, and rejoiced in Him in her spirit. What does that mean?

Our souls are our conscious minds, our personality and emotions. Our spirits are the part of us with which we commune with God. When something is magnified, it becomes larger in our vision. Then we see it more clearly. When we magnify God, we allow Him to increase in our vision, so we see His greatness more clearly. "O magnify the Lord with me," sings King David in Psalm 34:3, "and let us exalt His Name together . . ." (KJV) To extol God means to praise Him, to boast in Him with our mouth. "I will extol the Lord at all times; His praise will continually be on my lips," says Psalm 34:1.

When *we* worship God, we should "give it all we've got," just as Mary did.

Then we can say with the psalmist, "How good it is to . . . praise . . . our God!" (147:1)

Prayer: Lord, I want to worship You with everything I am and with all I have. I want to worship You in spirit and truth.

Day 15

For more understanding:

To learn more about why right worship is so important, you can read:

- that God does not honor *worship* that is not sincere (Matthew 15:8-9)
- that *worship* based on human commands and teaching doesn't honor God (Col. 2:23, Amplified)
- that God answers prayers when we *worship* Him with our whole heart (Psalm 138:1-3)

To learn more about how to please God with our worship, you can read:

- that our *worship* must be governed by God's Spirit, not by a desire to glorify ourselves (Philippians 3:3)
- that we should *worship* God with an attitude of reverence and awe toward His Greatness (Psalm 5:7, Amplified)
- that our *worship* should be full of rejoicing for God's goodness to us (Deut. 26:10-11)

To learn more about what happens to us when we have an attitude of continual worship, you can read:

- that God stores up His goodness for those who *continually worship* Him (Psalm 31:19, Amplified)
- that God is near us when our mouths are filled with *continual praise* (Psalm 71:8,12)
- that we present an acceptable sacrifice to God when His *praise* is *continually* on our lips (Hebrews 13:15)

Day 16

Celebrate!

Bible Subject: Rejoicing in God; Worship

Today's Reading: Luke 1:46-55

Today's Verse: "My spirit rejoices in God my Savior . . . for the Mighty One has done great things for me." (NIV and Amplified)

Today's Lesson: *Mary celebrated God for who He is and for His blessings to her.*

Birthdays, weddings, anniversaries, holidays—how we women love to celebrate! We love to decorate for special occasions, bake wonderful cakes, scour the Internet for just the right favors and games for that baby shower or children's party. There is something within us that loves to rejoice!

God made us that way. He gave women spirits that yearn for celebration and joy. He delights in our celebrations for family and friends, but most of all, He delights when we celebrate *Him*! Celebrating God is an important part of our worship. It's the part that comes most easily to us as women.

Mary's song brims and bubbles over with celebration of God. She celebrates God's character—His mercy (v. 50); His mighty deeds (v. 51); His provision (v. 53); His faithfulness (v. 48). She joys in God's blessings, both to her personally (vv. 48-49) and to His people (vv. 53-55).

We too can celebrate God. He wants us to! "Shout with joy, all the earth!" says Psalm 100. "Worship the Lord with gladness. Come before Him with joyful songs. It is He Who made us; we are His people, the sheep of His pasture" (vv. 1-3). In fact, the Bible tells us that we should go about our lives with a constant attitude of celebration in our hearts. "Rejoice in the Lord always," says Philippians 4:4. "Again I say rejoice!"

And did you know that God celebrates *us*? The Bible says "the Lord thy God will rejoice over thee with joy. He will rest in His love, He will joy over thee with singing" (Zephaniah 3:17, KJV). God loves us so much that He sings for joy when He thinks of us! Imagine that!

We should do the same for Him!

Prayer: Lord God, I celebrate you for all You are and all You've done for me. Help me keep an attitude of celebration all day long.

Day 16

For more understanding:

To learn more about celebrating God, you can read:

- that God's Word can be the *joy and rejoicing* of our hearts (Jeremiah 15:16)
- that we can *rejoice* in God's unfailing love toward us (Psalm 32:10-11)
- that the Lord Himself is our *Song* (Exodus 15:2)

To learn more about having a constant attitude of joy, you can read:

- that God makes each day for us to *rejoice* and be glad (Psalm 118:24)
- that putting our faith in God causes us to overflow with *joy* and hope (Romans 15:13, Amplified)
- that it is God's will that we be *joyful* always (1 Thessalonians 5:16-17)

To learn more about how God celebrates us, you can read:

- that all of heaven *rejoices* each time one person comes to God (Luke 15:7)
- that God *rejoices* in every creature He has made, including us (Psalm 104:30-31)
- that God *rejoices* over doing good for us (Jeremiah 32:40-41)

Day 17

The Ultimate Awesome

Bible Subject: Reverence; Fear of God

Today's Reading: Luke 1:46-55; Job 38:1-42:6

Today's Verse: "For the Mighty One has done great things for me; holy is His name. His mercy extends to those who fear Him from generation to generation." (Luke 1:49-50)

Today's Lesson: *Mary had a sense of awe for the Greatness of God and knew her complete dependence on Him.*

Awesome! If you know kids over the age of five, you probably hear that word a lot. Whether it's the "hottest" toy, the latest video game, or the cutest outfit at the mall, when they call it awesome, you can bet on two things: it's something they "gotta have," *and* it's something they think is better than everything else.

That's what Mary thought of God. When she speaks of "fearing" God (v. 50), she's saying that God is The Ultimate Awesome. Mary knew God was better than anything else she could ever desire, and that she *had* to have Him; she was utterly dependent on Him.

In the Bible, "fear of the Lord" means acknowledging that God is *awesome*. Another word for it is *reverence*. When we fear God or reverence Him, we give Him the honor He deserves because of His greatness and power. We recognize that He is the God of the whole universe, that He created everything—including us (Psalm 24:1). We understand our dependence on Him for everything, for the air we breathe, for the beating of our own hearts (Isaiah 42:5). We realize how much we need God's mercy and grace in our lives (Psalm 103:1-8).

It wasn't until Job understood the fear of God that he could truly experience God for himself (Job 42:1-5). That's why Proverbs 9:10 says, "The fear of the Lord is the *beginning* of wisdom." It's a starting point in our relationship with God.

Mary recognized that we can't *begin* to know God until we learn how to hold Him in awe. In fact, it's the very reason God made us! "Fear God; revere and worship Him," says Ecclesiastes 12:13, "for this is the full original purpose of our creation . . ." (Amplified Bible)

God is so awesome, He's the best thing we could ever want. Gotta have Him!

Prayer: Dear God, You are so awesome. Help me remember that I depend on You.

Day17

For more understanding:

To learn more about the benefits of fearing God, you can read:

- that God's mercy and loving-kindness are with those who *fear Him* (Psalm 103:17)
- that *reverential fear of God* helps us live lives consecrated to Him (2 Corinthians 7:1, Amplified)
- that *a reverential, worshipful attitude toward God* gives us peace of mind (Proverbs 19:23, Amplified)

To learn more about God's greatness and power, you can read:

- that God is the *only* One who has the *power* to do wonders and miracles (Psalm 136:4)
- that God uses His *incomparably great power* to benefit believers (Ephesians 1:18-19)
- that God's *greatness* makes Him alone worthy to be exalted as Ruler of over all things (1 Chronicles 29:11-12)

To learn more about dependence on God, you can read:

- that we can *depend on* God to be our Help when there is no one else to depend on (Psalm 121:1)
- that God stands at the right hand of those who acknowledge their *dependence on* Him (Psalm 109:31)
- that believers can confidently *depend on* receiving God's grace and mercy when we're in need (Hebrews 4:16)

Day 18

Humble Pie

Bible Subjects: Humility; Our Need for God

Today's Reading: Luke 1:46-55; Revelation 3:14-18

Today's Verse: "He has been mindful of the humble state of His servant." (Luke 1:48)

Today's Lesson: *Mary knew how much she needed God.*

My favorite children's book is *Charlotte's Web*. In it, Charlotte, a spider, saves the life of Wilbur the pig by spinning descriptive words about him into her web. The first word she spins is "Humble." Why was Wilbur humble? Because he knew that he was helpless to save himself from someone's dinner table. He had to put his hope in Charlotte, even though she was the tiniest of creatures. Wilbur recognized his need for Charlotte. He knew his humble state.

Mary was humble because she recognized her need for *God*. In her song, Mary says that God has "satisfied the hungry with good things, and the rich he has sent away empty-handed, without a gift" (v. 53,

Amplified). Mary was hungry for God, and she knew God alone could satisfy her need.

But why does she say that God sends "the rich" away empty-handed?

This isn't referring to a person's *material* state so much as his *spiritual* state. When you're rich, your every need is supplied, because you have the money to pay for it. So a rich person here means someone who doesn't think they need anything, including God. That's why they leave empty-handed— because they don't bother to stretch out their hand to God to be filled.

When you're hungry, you know you have a need—for food. When you're humble, you also know you have a need—for God. The Bible says that every one of us desperately needs God (Isaiah 53:6). But if we let pride and self-satisfaction blind us to that need, we'll be like the "rich" in Mary's song—we'll go away empty-handed, without receiving the blessings God wants to give us.

When we're humble, we see ourselves as we really are—in desperate need of God.

Prayer: Lord, help me to know how much I need You. Give me a humble, thankful heart.

Day 18

For more understanding:

To learn more about how important it is to be humble, you can read:

- that we must *humble* ourselves like a little child to be "great" in God's eyes (Matthew 18:4)
- that God *requires* believers to live *humble* lives (Micah 6:8)
- that when we willingly *humble* ourselves, God "lifts us up" to be used by Him for his purposes (James 4:10)

To learn more about how to humble ourselves, you can read:

- that giving up all our worries and concerns to God helps us to be *humble* (1 Peter 5:6-7)
- that remembering all God has done for us keeps us *humble* (Deut. 8:16,18)
- that whoever *humbles* himself by becoming a servant of others exalts himself in God's eyes (Matthew 23:11-12)

To learn more about what happens to us when we allow pride to make us think we don't need God, you can read:

- that God sets Himself against those who are too full of *pride* to listen to Him (James 4:6)
- that someone who is full of *pride* has no room for God in his thoughts (Proverbs 10:4)
- that *pride* is one of the things that makes us "unclean" in the sight of God (Mark 7:22-23)

Day 19

Hurry Up and Wait

Bible Subjects: Waiting on God; Faithfulness of God

Today's Reading: Luke 1:29-45, 56; Genesis 18:10-15, 21:1-3; 1 Samuel 1:4-11, 19-20

Today's Verses: "Mary stayed with Elizabeth for about three months and then returned home." (Luke 1:56)

"Now the Lord was gracious to Sarah as He had said, and the Lord did for Sarah what He had promised." (Genesis 21:1)

". . . The Lord remembered [Hannah]. So in the course of time Hannah conceived and gave birth to a son . . ." (1 Samuel 1:19b-20)

Today's Lesson: *Mary trusted God enough to patiently wait for Him to do everything He had promised her.*

Three women. Three promises from God for a child.

Two women—Sarah and Hannah—had prayed for many years to have a baby. Their prayers had seemingly gone unanswered.

One woman—Mary—was promised a baby that she had not even dreamed of having. Yet all three women had to wait on God. All three women had to trust God to bring about the fulfillment of His promise to them. They had to trust God for the details of how His promise would work out.

Mary particularly must have wondered how God would do what He promised. After she received the promise from God that she would have a baby who was God's own Son, Mary hurried to her cousin Elizabeth's house (vv.39-40), where she stayed for three months (v. 56). First she had to hurry; then she had to wait.

How long those months of waiting must have seemed to her, with thoughts swirling through her mind about what would happen to her when she went home with her pregnancy obvious to everyone. But Mary knew one thing for sure: God would be faithful to her. So she patiently waited on Him, trusting Him to work things out in his perfect timing in His perfect way.

The Bible says that God is faithful to *all* those who put their trust in Him (Psalm 5:11, Amplified). That means us! Whether we've been seeking God for years for an answer to prayer, or whether He promises us something that we've never even thought to pray for, we can be sure that He will be faithful in keeping His Word to us, however long we have to wait (Heb. 10:23).

When we wait on God, we learn to trust in His faithfulness. And God's faithfulness *never* fails (2 Tim. 2:15).

Prayer: God, help me trust You enough to wait. Help me to remember Your timing is perfect and Your ways are best.

Day 19

For more understanding:

To learn more about God's faithfulness, you can read:

- that God is *faithful to* take care of those who put their trust in Him (Psalm 5:11)
- that God's *faithfulness* is constant, everlasting, and unfailing (Lamentations 3:23)
- that God is *faithful* to give us the strength we need to wait on Him (1 Cor. 1:7-9)

To learn more about waiting upon God, you can read:

- that God answers our cry when we *wait on Him* (Psalm 40:1)
- that God acts on behalf of those who earnestly *wait on Him* (Isaiah 64:4)
- that God gives us the ability to *wait patiently for Him* to fulfill the hope we have in Him (Romans 8:25)

To learn more about how God fulfills His promises to us, you can read:

- that the greatest *Promise* God ever made to us was to send His Son to pay the penalty for our sins so we could have a relationship with God (Galatians 3:14)
- that God rewards us when we have confidence in His *promises* (Hebrews 10:35-36)
- that God's *promises* never fail (1 Kings 8:59)

Day 20

God's Game Plan

Bible Subjects: Trusting God in Difficult Circumstances; God's Plans for Us

Today's Reading: Matthew 1:18-25; Luke 1:26-45, 56

Today's Verse: "Now the birth of Jesus took place under these circumstances: When his mother Mary had been promised in marriage to Joseph, before they came together, she was found to be pregnant . . ." (Matthew 1:18, Amplified Bible)

Today's Lesson: *Mary had to trust in God's faithfulness to her during difficult circumstances.*

Mary was pregnant, and she was single.

Talk about difficult circumstances. At best, Mary would be shunned by the entire community. At worst, she'd be stoned. When the angel told Mary she'd give birth to the Son of God (Luke 1:32), he didn't say anything about a husband. Mary had no assurance that her fiancé Joseph would believe her story—or that anyone would. She had nothing to trust in except God's faithfulness to her and to the promise He had given her.

As she walked home from her cousin Elizabeth's house (Luke 1:56), Mary was three months pregnant, and probably beginning to show. Her heart must have been heavy with dread, knowing what people would think, knowing what Joseph would think. If *anyone* believed her, she must've told herself, *surely* Joseph would.

But he didn't. Not at first. Instead, Joseph broke off their engagement. Then he went home and went to bed.

Can you imagine the emotional agony Mary must have gone through during that long, lonely night? She must have wondered how she would ever be able to face her future alone. Mary had no way of knowing that that very night, God was taking care of her problem. That in the morning, Joseph would come to her and tell her that he'd had a dream from God, and *now* he believed her.

God is always faithful to us. Even when things are going wrong. Even when the plan that we thought He had for us doesn't seem to be working out the way we thought it would.

God's game plan is different from ours. God always has our spiritual best in mind, and sometimes that means that we must walk through difficult circumstances, like Mary did. God sees the end of the game from the beginning. We don't, so we have to put our trust in His faithfulness. He won't fail us!

Prayer: God, sometimes it's just so hard to trust You in the middle of a difficult time. Please help me remember Your faithfulness and Your promises even in my darkest moments. Help me trust Your game plan.

Day 20

For more understanding:

To learn more about how God helps us in difficult circumstances, you can read:

- that God gives us His strength to make it through *difficult times* (Phil. 3:14)
- that God's grace is all we need to get through *difficult circumstances* (2 Corin. 12:9)
- that God can give us great joy even though we're in the *worst of circumstances* (Habakkuk 3:17-19)

To learn more about how God always desires our spiritual best, you can read:

- that God uses trials to bring about our *spiritual health and welfare* (Phil. 1:19, Amp.)
- that God wants to build us up *spiritually* as if we were living stones (1 Tim 2:5)
- that God wants us to be *spiritually-minded* because that's how we find life and peace in Christ (Romans 8:6-11)

To learn more about how God never fails us, you can read:

- that God *never grows tired* of giving His strength to us when we need it (Isaiah 40:28-29)
- that God's love for us *never fails* (Lamentations 3:22)
- that Jesus is *always living* to pray for us (Hebrews 7:25)

Day 21

What's Going On Here?

Bible Subjects: God's Purposes; God's Timing; Trusting God

Today's Reading: Luke 2:1-7

Today's Verse: "While they were there, the time came for the baby to be born, and [Mary] gave birth to her firstborn. She wrapped Him in clothes and placed Him in a manger, because there was no room for them in the inn . . ." Luke 2:6-7

Today's Lesson: *Mary did her best to cooperate with God's plans, even though she didn't understand them.*

Babies don't wait. When the time comes for them to be born, they *come*.

What was Mary thinking that night, when she and Joseph had settled down in the hay beside the cows and donkeys, the smell of dung in the air, and her labor pains began? I know what *I* would've been thinking: Hey, wait a minute, God. *This* can't be right. You *can't* mean for my baby to be born *here*, in a *barn*. There must be some mistake!

But God doesn't make mistakes.

Mary knew that. She knew Him well enough to be sure that He knew what He was doing, even if she didn't. Maybe she didn't understand *why* her baby had to be born in a stable, but she accepted that God must have a reason for it. She may not have understood God's timing, but she did her best to cooperate with it.

Mary did what any mother would do for her baby. She made him warm and comfortable, and put him to bed. Then she trusted God to do the rest.

When we don't understand why things are happening the way they are in our lives, we need to remind ourselves that God is in control. The Bible says that our steps are determined by God, and it's He who makes them sure (Proverbs 16:9). This means that God has a good reason for what He does in our lives, and it's meant for our benefit (Romans 8:28).

When we don't understand what's going on, we have to trust in the One who does. "I have set the Lord always before me," says Psalm 37:8. "Because He is at my right hand, I will not be shaken." Like Mary, we need to cooperate with God's timing and purposes the best way we know how, and leave the rest up to Him.

Prayer: Oh, Lord, help me to remember that Your ways are best and that I can trust You even when things don't make sense.

Day 21

For more understanding:

To learn more about how to cooperate with God's timing, you can read:

- that Jesus tells us to be alert and watchful so that we'll recognize *God's timing* (John 13:33-37)
- that wise hearts (spiritual understanding) help us discern *God's timing* (Ecclesiastes 8:5-6)
- that submitting ourselves to God's authority allows us to cooperate with *His timing* (2 Peter 5:6)

To learn more about why God never makes mistakes, you can read:

- that God is *perfect* (Matthew 5:48)
- that God's way is *perfect* and His Word is *flawless* (Psalm 18:30)
- that God is *unequaled in* the *rightness* of His ways (Psalm 71:19)

To learn about why we can't expect to fully understand God's plans for us, you can read:

- that God's *decisions* are unfathomable and His *methods* undiscoverable (Romans 11:33, Amplified Bible)
- that God's *understanding* is limitless and beyond our ability to comprehend (Isaiah 40:13, 28)
- that our minds are darkened to *spiritual understanding* unless Himself grants it to us (Ephesians 1:18, 4:18)

Day 22

Hidden Treasure

Bible Subjects: Living by God's Word

Today's Reading: Luke 2:8-20

Today's Verse: "Mary treasured all these things and pondered them in her heart." (Luke 2:19)

Today's Lesson: Mary recognized how vital God's Word was to her life

Our children are special to us. From the moment we're born, we treasure everything they do, everything they say, and everything everyone else says about them.

Even before Jesus was born, Mary heard some amazing things concerning who He would be and what He would do. Now that she had held her precious baby in her arms, she must have been pinching herself, wondering if everything she had heard about her tiny son could really be true. Then the shepherds came. When they told Mary what *they* had seen and heard about Jesus, Mary must have known with absolute certainty that it *was* true. All of it. Everything God said would happen was happening *now*—to *her*, and to her son.

What *things* was Mary treasuring in verse 19 above? I believe it was the Word of God, coming true before her very eyes! The Bible says that God's Word is better than much silver and gold (Psalm 119:72). When we read that Mary "pondered [these things]" in her heart, we can imagine that she was thinking about God's Word over and over, trying to remember it. She knew that, as she reared her son, she would need the wisdom and guidance that God gives through His Word.

Just as we do. Understanding God's Word is like having riches, Paul says in

Colossians 2:2-3, and the wisdom and knowledge we gain from knowing God's Word is our "treasure." We're supposed to hide the treasure of God's Word in our hearts (Psalm 119:11)—to ponder it as Mary did, to think on it, memorize it, and make it a part of our lives.

Imagine . . . God's Word is our hidden treasure! His Words are just as vital to us today, as they were when Moses said to the Israelites so long ago: "They are not just idle words for you—they are your life." (Deut. 32:47)

Prayer: Lord, help me to treasure Your life-giving Word. Help me to read it and think on it every day and realize how vital it is to me.

Day 22

For more understanding:

To learn more about the benefits of knowing God's Word, you can read:

- that *knowing God's Word* equips us for doing God's work (2 Tim. 3:16-17)
- *knowing God's Word* gives us wisdom upon which we can build our lives (Proverbs 23:3-4, Amplified)
- that *knowing God's Word* builds our faith (Acts 20:32)

To learn more about how important it is to understand God's Word, you can read:

- that *understanding* His Word is like a light to our minds that gives us wisdom we would not ordinarily have (Psalm 119:130, 19:7)
- that *spiritual understanding* helps us live a life worthy of the Lord (Colossians 1:9)
- that through *understanding of His Word* God reveals to us the true thoughts and motives of our own hearts (Hebrews 4:12)

To learn more about how to understand God's Word, you can read:

- that God gives *understanding* of His Word to anyone who asks Him for it (James 1:5)
- that Jesus can give believers *insight* into the Word (Luke 24:45)
- that God grants *wisdom and discernment* to those who ask for it (1 Kings 3:12)

Day 23

Come and Worship!

Bible Subjects: Worship

Today's Reading: Matthew 2:1-12

Today's Verse: "[The Magi] saw the Child with His mother Mary, and they bowed down and worshiped Him. Then they opened their treasures and presented him with gifts of gold, incense, and myrrh." (Matthew 2:11)

Today's Lesson: *Mary was eager to give God the kind of worship He desires.*

The purpose of the Magi's visit to Mary's home was worship—to worship Jesus, the Son of God. But because Jesus was so young, probably only a toddler, Mary would have been right there beside him when the Magi opened their treasures to Him. Gold, incense, and myrrh—real treasures, but likely symbolic of spiritual treasures as well.

Many things in the Bible have double meanings—both natural or "real" meanings, and symbolic meanings.* Often the symbolic meanings can be discovered from seeing what else the Bible has to say about that subject. This, I believe, is true of the treasures the Magi brought to Jesus.

About worship, the Bible says, "The reverent fear and worship of the Lord is your treasure and His" (Isaiah 33:6, Amplified). True worship is something God greatly values (John 4:23), and the Magi's treasures could well be representative of what God wanted to teach Mary—and us—about a better way to worship Him. Through Jesus, God was going to present a new way of worship to His people—a worship that was internal rather than external.** Each gift that was laid before Jesus could symbolize one aspect of the kind of worship God desires.

Gold could symbolize knowledge of God's Word. Says Psalm 19:8-9: "The [words] of the Lord . . . are more precious than gold, than much pure gold." Frankincense could depict prayer. "May my prayer be set before you like incense," says Psalm 141:21. Myrrh was used to make the sacred anointing oil used in the Tabernacle for consecration of people and things to God (Exodus 30:22, 29). Thus, the gift of myrrh could represent the lives of consecration and holiness that God desires from believers. The Bible says that through Christ we can serve as priests to God Himself (Rev. 1:6)!

What a wonderful way to worship our God!

Prayer: Lord, You are my King. You are so worthy of all my gifts of worship. Help me worship You as You deserve.

Harper's Bible Dictionary, p. 1004
**Harper's Bible Dictionary*, p. 1146

Day 23

For more understanding:

To learn more about how gold or riches can represent God's Word, you can read:

- that wisdom from God's Word is better than *choice gold, rubies, or pearls* (Prov. 8:8-11, Amplified)
- that the Gospel of Christ is *wealth* beyond our human understanding (Ephesians 3:8)
- that God's Word is better than *thousands of pieces of gold or silver* (Psalm 119:72)

To learn more about how incense can represent prayers of faith, you can read:

- that the prayers of believers, like smoke from *incense,* go up straight to God's throne (Rev. 8:3-4)
- that the prayers of believers are like *incense* offered to God in golden bowls (Revelation 5:8)
- that our prayers are like *incense* set before God (Psalm 141:2)

To learn more about how "anointing" can represent consecration to God, you can read:

- that being *anointed* with myrrh can set someone apart from other people (Psalm 45:7)
- that believers receive an *anointing* from Christ that allows us to lead lives consecrated to Him (1 John 2:27)
- that through Christ, God *anoints* us as His and sets His seal of ownership upon us (1 Corinthians 1:21-22)

Day 24

God's On-the-Job Training

Bible Subjects: Ministry; God's Purpose for Us

Today's Reading: Luke 2:21-40

Today's Verse: "... a sword will pierce your own soul, too." (Luke 2:35)

Today's Lesson: *God prepared Mary ahead of time for the ministry that He had chosen for her.*

The days after the birth of a child are a special time in a mother's life. For hours on end we gaze in unbelief at the miracle that is our tiny son or daughter. Mary too must have spent the first week of Jesus' life marveling at her newborn son. Even though she knew He was the Son of God, Jesus was *her* son too—*her* baby. In her mind, Mary knew that Jesus was the Messiah, yet in her mother's heart, surely she would have treasured him as her own.

God in His mercy allowed Mary a week to think of Jesus this way. Then He had to gently remind her that Jesus didn't belong to her. God had given Mary a ministry to mother His Son, and He had to begin preparing her. As Jesus' mother, Mary would have to face many difficult and painful situations, many "swords" that would pierce her soul. The most agonizing would be witnessing Jesus' death on the cross.

Up until that day at the Temple, Mary had heard many wonderful prophecies about Jesus—from Gabriel, Elizabeth, Zechariah, and the shepherds. Simeon's words to Mary were different. Through Simeon's prophecy, God began to prepare Mary for the opposition and persecution that Jesus would face—and that Mary would witness. From then onward, Mary would have known that she had to begin releasing her son to God for the purpose for which God had sent Him. She also gained some insight into what her role in God's plan would be.

God never asks us to do anything for Him unless He first prepares us for it. The Bible says that God has made us *competent* as "ministers of a new covenant" (2 Corinthians 3:6). God makes sure we're well equipped for whatever job or ministry He has planned for us!

Prayer: Thank you, Lord, for preparing me for the ministry You have planned for me.

Day 24

For more understanding:

To learn more about how God equips for His work, you can read:

- that God's Word thoroughly *equips* us for every good work (2 Tim. 3:16)
- that God *equips* us with everything good for doing His will (Hebrew 3:20-21)
- that God *equips* his people for works of service (Ephesians 4:12)

To learn more about how God prepares us for what He asks us to do, you can read:

- that God makes us *fit and ready* to be used as instruments for His purposes (2 Tim. 2:21b, NIV and Amplified)
- that God has *specially made us* for the good works He planned in advance for us to do (Ephesians 2:10)
- that God *prepares* us beforehand to become His people (Romans 9:23-25)

To learn more about how *every* believer is a minister and has a ministry, you can read:

- that God gives all believers a *ministry* of reconciliation as ambassadors for Christ (2 Cor. 5:18)
- that we're supposed to *minister* to one another so we can all reach maturity in Christ (Ephesians 4:12-13, Amplified)
- that we are *ministers* whenever we serve the Lord by meeting the needs of others (Hebrews 6:10)

Day 25

Free for the Taking

Bible Subjects: Wisdom, Spiritual Understanding

Today's Reading: Luke 2:41-52

Today's Verse: "But [Mary and Joseph] did not understand what [Jesus] was saying to them." (Luke 2:50)

Today's Lesson: *Mary had to continually seek wisdom and understanding from God.*

Ask any parent of a teenager and they'll probably tell you the hardest thing about living with their son or daughter is *attitude*. Teenagers think they know it all.

But Jesus was a teenager who really *did* know it all. When Mary and Joseph found him in the Temple, Jesus was astounding the most knowledgeable men of the city—the religious leaders—with his understanding and answers. The Amplified Bible says that everyone who was listening was "astonished and overwhelmed with bewildered wonder," including His parents. For the last three days, Mary and Joseph had been frantic with worry over Jesus, and when they asked Him for an explanation, they didn't even understand His answer!

After this experience they would have been much more keenly aware of how much wisdom and guidance they needed from God to parent Jesus to adulthood. Mary and Joseph had to seek God every day for the wisdom they needed as the earthly parents of Jesus.

God wants us to seek wisdom from Him, too. Understanding from God is of great value. The Bible compares wisdom and understanding to money (Proverbs 23:23), an inheritance (Ecclesiastes 7:11), precious jewels (Proverbs 31:10, 26), and a house filled with rare and beautiful treasures (Proverbs 24:3-4).

Yet God gives it to us freely! All we have to do is ask Him for it. James 1:5 says, "If any of you lacks wisdom, [you] should ask God, who gives generously to all . . . and it will be given to [you]."

But it doesn't happen overnight. Growing in understanding is a process, and we have to do our part. In prayer, we ask God for understanding, and in our lives we seek it out, by studying His Word (Psalm 19:7), and by listening to God's voice speak to our hearts (Ephesians 3:10, 12).

We need God's wisdom in our lives. It's a treasure we can't live without!

Prayer: God, thank you that You give your wisdom and understanding so freely. I ask You for the wisdom and understanding I need for today.

Day 25

For more understanding:

To learn more about the wisdom that comes from God, you can read:

- that *God's wisdom* makes us more peace-loving, considerate, impartial and sincere (James 3:17)
- that *God's wisdom* gives us spiritual insight and helps us become acquainted with Him (Ephesians 1:17)
- that *God's wisdom* is proved right by the way we live our lives when we follow it (Matthew 11:19)

To learn more about the understanding that comes from God, you can read:

- that spiritual wisdom and *understanding* help us discern God's will for us (Col 1:9)
- that *understanding* is a fountain of life to those who have it (Proverbs 16:22)
- that God alone gives *understanding* (2 Tim. 2:7)

To learn more about how to get wisdom and understanding, you can read:

- that Jesus gives us *wisdom* that people won't be able to contradict (Luke 21:15)
- that God's Spirit gives us *wisdom* (1 Corinthians 12:8)
- that our *understanding* is darkened until God Himself illuminates it (Ephesians 4:18)

Day 26

Leave It To Me

Bible Subject: Hope, Trusting God

Today's Reading: John 2:1-11

Today's Verse: "Jesus said to her, 'Dear Woman, leave it to me . . .'" (John 2:4, Amplified)

Today's Lesson: *In a hopeless situation, Mary put her hope in Jesus.*

Weddings—a time of joy and celebration, when we want to do all we can to make things perfect, to create cherished memories for the bride and groom, family, and friends.

At the wedding in Cana, Mary wanted to do just that—make the wedding the best that it could be for everyone. It was likely the marriage of a family member or close family friend, since Jesus and his disciples were there. The bride or groom must have been someone special to Mary—perhaps even a younger sister or brother—for Mary to be so concerned about having no wine for the guests. In

Bible times, when showing hospitality was tied to a person's reputation, running out of wine would've been a family disgrace, and a great offense to all the guests.

But what could Mary do? She certainly couldn't produce more wine. The situation seemed hopeless, the wedding doomed, along with the family's reputation. And Mary was helpless to do anything about it.

Or was she? The Bible says, "Let us hold unswervingly to the hope we profess, for He who promised is faithful" (Hebrews 10:23). In her *own* strength, there was nothing Mary could do to bring hope to this hopeless situation. But she knew Jesus *could*. Jesus didn't tell her what He was going to do about the wine, or even that He was going to do anything at all. Mary simply held fast to the hope she had in Jesus, knowing He was faithful, and that was enough.

Mary took her need to Jesus, left it to Him, and trusted Him to take care of it. We can do the same. We don't have to know *how* Jesus will help us, just that He will.

Today, Jesus says to us the same thing that He said to Mary so long ago: Dear woman, leave it to Me.

Prayer: Lord, thank You for being concerned about things that concern me. Help me to take my concerns to You and leave them with You.

Day 26

For more understanding:

To learn more about hoping in God, you can read:

- that *hope in God* gives us a secure anchor to which we can hold (Hebrews 6:19)
- that those who *hope in the Lord* renew their strength (Isaiah 40:31)
- that we can put our *hope in God's* unfailing love (Psalm 147:11)

To learn more about how God gives us hope in hopeless situations, you can read:

- that God gives us the ability to *hope* for something we're not able to see (Romans 8:24)
- that God directs His love toward us to give us *hope* when we're downcast (Psalm 42:5,8)
- that *hope* in God enables us to be joyful in the midst of affliction (Romans 12:12)

To learn more about taking our needs to God, you can read:

- that God richly supplies our every *need* (1 Tim. 6:17)
- that God meets all our *needs* according to His riches in glory (Php. 4:19)
- that God promises to satisfy our *needs* (Isaiah 58:11)

Day 27

Get Involved

Bible Subject: Faith, Prayer, A Relationship with God

Today's Reading: John 2:1-11

Today's Verse: "'Dear Woman, why do you involve Me?' Jesus replied." (John 2:4)

Today's Lesson: *Mary focused more on her faith in Jesus than she did on a specific need in her life.*

The wedding in Cana was in trouble. The host had run out of wine, and Mary was one of the few people who knew about it. Without wine, the celebration would come to an abrupt end. All hope for the wedding seemed lost—unless Jesus could help. So Mary took the problem to Him.

On the surface, Jesus reply to Mary seems discouraging rather than hopeful. He doesn't promise to do *anything*. But a closer look reveals a deeper meaning to His words. He seems to be asking Mary for a moment of soul-searching. Perhaps He wants her to consider *why* she's bringing the request to Him. Is she seeking *only* to have a specific need met—wine for the wedding—or is she seeking something more significant? Is she more focused on the *need* she's bringing to Jesus, or on Jesus Himself?

The Bible tells us to seek *first* God's Kingdom and "His righteousness, His way of doing and being right, and then *all these things* . . . will be given you besides" (Matthew 6:33, Amplified). This means that we're supposed to focus more on our relationship with God than we are on what God can do for us. Yes, God does wants to meet our needs. But the most important thing God wants from us is faith. He tells us to bring our requests to Him in prayer, not just so He can give us what we want, but so that we can learn to trust Him (Philippians 4:6-7, 19).

That's what faith is.

We, too, must consider the question that Jesus asked Mary. Why should *we* involve God in our problems . . . and our lives? *Because God wants us to.* It's the very reason Jesus came. God wants to have a relationship with us—a relationship based on our faith in Who He is (Romans 5:8-11). Mary had it. We can, too!

Prayer: Thank you, Lord, that You want a relationship with me! Thank You that I can bring everything to You, no matter how big or how small.

Day 27

For more understanding:

To learn more about how to have a relationship with God, you can read:

- that Jesus's sacrifice of His own life on the cross justifies us so that can have a *relationship with God* (Romans 5:9)
- that our faith gives us righteousness in God's eyes and brings us into *right relationship with Him* (2 Cor. 5:21, Rom. 10:6)
- that Jesus makes God known to us, so that we can have a *relationship with Him* (John 1:18)

To learn more about the benefits of having a right relationship with God, you can read:

- that having a *right relationship with God* leads to peace and spiritual prosperity (Isaiah 58:8, Amplified)
- that a *relationship with God* based on faith gives us a spiritual fervor, or excitement, that we can't get any other way (Hebrews 10:38, Amplified)
- that a close *relationship with God* enables us to hear His voice clearly (John 10:26-28)

To learn more about trusting in our relationship with God, you can read:

- that we should *trust in our relationship with God* to get us through difficult times rather than getting discouraged at how hopeless our situation seems (2 Cor. 5:7, Amplified)
- that *trusting in our relationship with God* gives us strength and confidence (Isaiah 30:15, Amplified)
- that we're blessed when we *trust in our relationship with God* (Psalm 2:12)

Day 28

A Heavenly Landlord

Bible Subject: Prayer, God's Sovereignty, God's Timing and Purpose

Today's Reading: John 2:1-11

Today's Verse: "Dear Woman, what is that to you and Me? . . . My hour to act has not yet come." (John 2:4)

Today's Lesson: *Mary understood that God is in control of every situation.*

Ever signed a lease to rent a home? The lease gives the owner control over practically everything you do in the house. You may be living there, but the lease reminds you that the owner maintains sovereignty, or control, over his own property.

At Cana, something similar seems to be taking place in the conversation between Mary and Jesus. Mary comes to Jesus with a request for Him to intervene in a situation that concerns her: the hosts have run out of wine. Yet, instead of telling Mary how He's going to address her problem, Jesus seems to be asking her to think more carefully about what she's asking Him to do. He seems to be gently reminding her of God's *sovereignty*—that God has complete control over this situation, and *every* situation.

First, Jesus reassures Mary of His loving concern for her. He calls her Dear Woman, a term of respect and endearment.* Then He seems to ask her to consider the relationship between them, and the importance of her request in light of that. Perhaps He's reminding her that the primary relationship between them is a spiritual one, rather than just that of mother and son. Lastly, Jesus brings up timing, reminding Mary that God has a perfect time and a purpose for everything (Ecclesiastes 3:1).

Sometimes we, too, bring requests to God without much thought to what we're asking. We must remember that we're like renters in this world. Just as renters don't have a right to question how the property owner wants his property treated, we don't have the right to expect God to run His world the way we think He should. Yet God promises in His Word that whatever He does is for our spiritual benefit and welfare (Psalm 103:1-5, Philippians 1:19, Amplified).

What a relief that we can trust in a God who's in control!

Prayer: Heavenly Father, thank You for your loving concern for me. Help me to remember that You are sovereign, that You are in control, and that whatever You do is for my ultimate welfare.

---

*See John 2:4, Amplified Bible

Day 28

For more understanding:

To learn more about praying with God's sovereignty in mind, you can read:

- that Jesus teaches us to remember when we pray that *God is in control of everything* (Luke 11:2b)
- that God wants us to remember when we pray that He is *in control of every situation*
- (1 Thessalonians 5:17-18, Amplified) that we should praise God in our prayers because *His power and understanding have no limit* (Psalm 147:1,5)

To learn more about praying with God's timing and purpose in mind, you can read:

- that Jesus Himself prayed according to *God's will and purpose* (Matthew 26:39)
- that we can be confident in prayer when we ask things in agreement with *God's own plan* (1 John 5:14)
- that God's own Spirit helps us pray in agreement with *His will and purpose* (Romans. 8:26-27)

To learn more about trusting every situation to God, you can read:

- that God is reliable and *trustworthy* and He can be depended on (1 Cor. 1:9, Amplified)
- that God is on the lookout for opportunities to come to our rescue when we *trust in Him* (2 Chronicles 16:9)
- that God's unfailing love for us means we can *trust Him* to come to our rescue (Psalm 6:4)

Day 29

Our Father's Business

Bible Subject: Faith, Prayer, God's Timing

Today's Reading: John 2:1-11, Luke 2:40-52

Today's Verse: "'You and I see things differently,' Jesus replied." (John 2:4a, Holman Christian Standard Bible)

"Did you not see and know that it is necessary for Me to be . . . occupied [with] My Father's business?" (Luke 2:49, Amplified)

Today's Lesson: *Mary realized that God's first order of business is increasing our faith.*

Mary was the mother of Jesus, but she was also human—like us. As humans, we're prone to think of things in natural terms, what we can see, hear, and touch. When we think of time, we think of the next hour, or the next day, or what will happen next month, or next year. But God is Spirit. His viewpoint is spiritual—always. He sees time differently, too: from an eternal perspective. One day with God is like a thousand years. That's why, to us, it may seem sometimes that God acts far too slowly—or not at all (2 Peter 3:8). When Mary brought her problem to Jesus—no wine at the wedding—no doubt she wanted Jesus to take care of it right away. But Jesus had to remind her of God's spiritual and eternal perspective. More than anything, Mary needed to trust Jesus. Her immediate problem was not the first order of business with Jesus. Her faith was.

God see things differently than we do. Our everyday problems are important to Him, but not nearly as important as our faith. God is in the faith-building business. Building our faith is always His first concern.

We must remember this when we pray. Just because God doesn't immediately resolve a situation doesn't mean He's not going to take care of it at all. Jesus did take care of Mary's problem. But He did it in *His* way in *His* time. His way turned out to be a miracle—He changed water into wine. And because He did it His way, the Bible says that all His disciples put their faith in Him (John 2:11). When we trust God to do things His way on His timetable, faith is the result. And faith is the best thing that could possibly happen to us. May we, like Jesus' disciples, cry out to God: "Lord, increase our faith!" (Luke 17:5)

Prayer: Dear Father, help me to look at things from a spiritual perspective rather than a natural one. Teach me to trust You so that my faith can grow.

Day 29

For more understanding:

To learn more about why faith is God's first priority, you can read:

- that it is through *faith* in Christ that we receive salvation (Gal. 2:20)
- that without faith it's impossible to please God (Hebrews 11:6)
- that *faith* makes us righteous in God's eyes (Romans 5:1; Gal. 2:16, 3:24)

To learn more about the benefits of faith, you can read:

- that having *faith* allows God's power to work in our lives (Matt. 9:29, Mark 11:22-23, Luke 7:9, Acts 14:9)
- faith can give us confidence and boldness as we serve Christ (1 Tim. 3:13, Amplified)
- that our *faith* encourages us and others (Romans 1:12)

To learn more about seeing things from God's spiritual, eternal perspective, you can read:

- that God's own Spirit can help us understand some things from *God's perspective* (John 16:13, 1 Cor. 2:10-12)
- that God's Spirit teaches us about Him and reminds us of His Words so that we can better see things from *His perspective* (John 14:26)
- that seeing from *God's perspective* means we must accept that some of God's ways are simply beyond our limited understanding (Romans 11:33-36)

Day 30

Lean on God

Bible Subject: Faith, Believing God, Trust

Today's Reading: John 2:1-11

Today's Verse: "'Whatever He says to You, do it.'" (John 2:5, Amplified)

Today's Lesson: *Mary trusted Jesus completely, and acted on her faith in Who He was.*

There was no wine left at the wedding in Cana. When Mary asked Jesus what to do about it, His reply didn't seem to offer much hope for a solution to the problem. Yet Mary held fast to her faith in Who Jesus was and remained fully confident that He would take care of the situation. Mary was so sure of Jesus' help that she instructed the servants to do whatever He said, even though He hadn't promised to do a thing!

The Bible tells us to draw near to God in *full assurance of faith*, "in unqualified assurance and absolute conviction, by leaning of our entire personality on God, [putting] absolute trust and confidence in His power, wisdom, and goodness." (Hebrews 10:22, Amplified).

When we "lean" on God, we "give Him all we've got." We trust Him so much that we put our absolute and total dependence in His character—in who He is. Then we put our faith into action. This is what Mary did at Cana.

Mary had full assurance of faith that all she had to do was make a need known to Jesus, and then do whatever He said. Mary *believed*, and then she acted on her belief. As a result of her faith, Jesus performed His first miracle.

Think of it! Jesus' first miracle was based on the faith of one woman!

"Truly I tell you," Jesus says in Matthew 17:20, "if you have faith as small as a mustard seed, you can say to this mountain, 'Move from here to there,' and it will move. Nothing will be impossible for you." If we can do nothing else in a situation, at least we can believe God! "Everything is possible for one who believes," Jesus says in Mark 9:21.

Faith is a choice we make. Let's make the same choice Mary made. Whatever God says to us, let's do it!

Prayer: God, You are a God of miracles! Give me full assurance of faith and help me choose to believe.

Day 30

For more understanding:

To learn more about full assurance of faith, you can read:

- that through *faith* we allow Christ to have predominance in our hearts (Ephesians 3:17)
- that *faith* is the confidence that what we hope for will actually happen (Hebrews 11:1)
- that *faith* means we serve God wholeheartedly (2 Chronicles 19:9)

To learn more about why acting on our faith is so important, you can read:

- that *acts prompted by our faith* help us fulfill God's purposes (2 Thess. 1:11)
- that our *acts of faith* promote God's work (1 Tim. 1:4)
- that *faith* without accompanying action is dead and useless (James 2:20)

To learn more about what happens when we put total trust in God, you can read:

- that God will never disappoint us when we *trust Him completely* (Psalm 25:2)
- that *absolute trust in God* gives us understanding about His Word (2 Tim. 3:15)
- that God keeps us from fear when we *rely confidently on Him* (Psalm 56:4, Amp.)

Day 31

Terrible Times

Bible Subject: Drawing Near to God, Difficult Circumstances

Today's Reading: John 19:1-30

Today's Verse: "Near the cross of Jesus stood His mother." (John 19:25)

Today's Lesson: *In the worst time of her life, Mary stayed near Jesus.*

It was here—the worst nightmare of Mary's life. Her son was dying, and Mary was right beside him, witnessing all His suffering. The fact that she had known it would happen someday did not lesson the blow, or ease the agony she felt. Mary knew that there was only one way she could get through this terrible time, and that was to come close to Jesus, and stay there. That's what she did.

That's what we must do also, when our terrible times come. No one who has ever lived has been immune from pain and suffering, or the terror of sudden tragedy. Yet even in the midst of our own personal nightmares, God is there. He is our Refuge, so we don't have to be afraid (Psalm 91:1-6).

When the agonies of life come to us, we must face them— by drawing near to God, like Mary did. When we do that, He draws near to us (James 4:8). Not only does He promise to help us in our terrible times, He comes *running* to do it. "But You O Lord, be not far off," Psalm 22:19 says, "Come quickly to help me."

God takes care of us in our terrible times, like a shepherd takes care of his sheep. Isaiah 40:11 says, "He gathers the lambs in His arms, and carries them close to His heart." What a wonderful promise! When our hearts are breaking, God holds us close to His own heart, and carries us. He gets us through. He gives us His own Spirit to comfort us in our sorrow and pain (John 14:16, Isaiah 61:2).

In the worst times of our life, we can turn to Jesus. Jesus promised that He would not leave us "comfortless, desolate, bereaved, forlorn, or helpless" (John 14:18, Amplified). How thankful we can be that our God is "the Father of compassion and the Source of every comfort"! (2 Corinthians 1:3, Amplified).

Prayer: Dear Lord, help me to draw close to You and stay close to You, especially when everything around me is falling apart. In the dark and terrible times, please let me know that You are near.

Day 31

For more understanding:

To learn more about how God is with us in the worst times of our lives, you can read:

- that no matter where we go, *God is with us*, holding us in His hand (Psalm 139:7-10)
- that *God is an ever-present help* in times of trouble (Psalm 46:1)
- that *God is with us* in the darkest and most hopeless times of our lives (Psalm 23:4)

To learn more about how we can draw near to God in the worst times of our lives, you can read:

- that we *draw near to God* by putting our trust in Him (Psalm 73:28)
- that we *draw near to God* by asking Him to help us understand His Word (Psalm 119:169)
- that we *draw near to God* by leaning on Him with absolute faith in His power, wisdom, and goodness (Heb. 10:22, Amp.)

To learn more about how God gives us comfort when we need it, you can read:

- that God's protection and guidance gives us *comfort* (Psalm 23:4, Amplified)
- that God *comforts* us when we're down-hearted (2 Corinthians 7:6)
- that God Himself says He is the One Who *comforts* us (Isaiah 51:12)

Day 32

Our Caretaker

Bible Subject: God's Loving Care, Trusting God

Today's Reading: John 19:1-30

Today's Verse: "When Jesus saw His mother there and the disciple whom He loved standing nearby, He said to [her], "Dear woman, here is your son . . ." (John 19:26)

Today's Lesson: *In the worst time of her life, Mary trusted Jesus to take care of her.*

Women are caretakers. God has put in our hearts the desire to nurture and attend to the needs of those we love. Whether it's our children, an ailing spouse or aging parents, a friend in need or a beloved animal, we women have a natural inclination to want to tend to those who need help or attention.

God is a care-taker too. We see God's loving care for us in the way that Jesus provided for the needs of His mother, even as He was dying on the cross. Since Mary was a widow,* Jesus, as the eldest son, would have been responsible for her. In the midst of His own agony, we're told that Jesus "saw" Mary, which means He paid attention to her, or looked after her.** For Mary, witnessing Jesus being crucified was probably the worst thing she could ever imagine happening to her. Jesus made certain she knew that she would be taken care of, even though He would not be physically there Himself to do it.

God wants us to know that He sees *us* in the midst of our very worst times—and He promises to take care of us (Psalm 25:18). "Cast your burden on the Lord, releasing the weight of it, and He will sustain you," says Psalm 55:12 (Amplified). God delights to pay attention to us and care for us, as a mother hen cares for her chicks (Luke 13:34). He has compassion on us like parents have compassion on their children (Psalm 103:13). Jesus said, "In the world you will have tribulation, but be of good cheer. I have overcome the world!" (John 16:33).

In the midst of our afflictions, God is there, remembering us and taking care of us perfectly!

Prayer: Dear Lord, how I thank you for your promises to take care of me. Help me remember You love me, no matter what I am going through.

---

*According to Smith's Bible Names Dictionary, Joseph had most likely died by the time of Jesus' crucifixion.

**The word translated as "saw" in John 19:26 is the Hebrew word *har*, which is transliterated as "ra'ah." It can mean "to give attention to" or to "look after." (biblestudytools.com/lexicons/hebrew)

Day 32

For more understanding:

To learn more about why we can trust God during our terrible times, you can read:

- that no one who trusts in the Lord *when in trouble* shall be left desolate (Psalm 34:22, KJV)
- that God's unfailing love surrounds and protects us *in times of trouble* (Ps. 32:7,10)
- that God is our refuge *in disaster* (Jeremiah 17:7,17)

To learn more about how God helps us during our terrible times, you can read:

- that God watches over us during *difficult times* and keeps us from harm (Psalm 121)
- that God is our strength and ever-present help in *times of trouble* (Psalm 46:1)
- that we can call upon God's mercy and grace to help us in *times of need* (Heb. 4:16)

To learn more about God's loving concern for us, you can read:

- that God cares about us affectionately and watchfully (1 Peter 5:7, Amp.)
- that Jesus cares for us so much He gave His life for us (John 10:11, 15:13)
- that, while we were still lost in our sins, God poured out His loving concern for us by giving us a Saviour (Rom. 5:5-6, Amp.)

Day 33

Best Friends Forever

Bible Subject: Prayer, God's Presence in Difficult Times, God's Friendship

Today's Reading: John 19:25-27, Acts 1:1-14

Today's Verse: "They all joined together constantly in prayer." (Acts 1:14)

Today's Lesson: *During a terrible time in her life, Mary prayed.*

Do you have a best friend? A friend whom you can always talk to, who always understands, and who knows you better than you know yourself? A true friend is someone who stands with us and shares the worst times of our life, as well the best times. "A friend loves at all times," says Proverbs 17:17.

The best friend we could ever have is God. Mary knew this. That's why, during the worst time of her life, she talked to God in prayer. Mary had just witnessed the agonizing death of her son Jesus. Her husband was dead, and she had no home of her own.* Her pain and grief must have seemed unbearable, and her future bleak. So Mary prayed.

Mary knew from watching Jesus for 33 years that her only hope to get through this terrible time was to talk to her best friend—God. The Bible tells us that the prayers of His people are precious to God (Psalm 142:2). When we choose to have a relationship with God, we become God's friends (John 15:15). And because we're His friends, God's eyes and ears are continually focused on us (1 Peter 3:12). That means He is always listening to us!

In the terrible times of our own lives, we can pray, and cry out to a Friend who promises to help us (Hebrews 13:6). When we're hurting, when we feel hopeless, alone, and afraid, we can talk to God. When we have no strength of our own, God gives us His. In our weakest and most vulnerable times, says 2 Cor. 12:9 (Amp), Christ Himself pitches a tent of His own strength over our heads and stays with us!

God is the only friend we could ever have who will never leave our side!

Prayer: Dear Lord, You are truly the best friend anyone could have. Thank You for the truth that You are always here for me and will never leave me.

*Mary had been sent to live with Jesus' close friend and disciple, John. (See John 19:26, 27.)

Day 33

For more understanding:

To learn more about why we should pray during our terrible times, you can read:

- that the first thing Jesus did in His terrible times was *pray* (Luke 22:44)
- that God promises to rescue us from our troubles when we cry out to Him in *prayer* (Psalm 34:17)
- that Jesus talks to the Father on our behalf when we ask Him to in *prayer* (Luke 22:32)

To learn more about how God stays close to us during terrible times, you can read:

- that the *Lord is close* to the broken-hearted and crushed in spirit (Psalm 34:18)
- that *God is nearer to us* when we're in trouble than are those who oppose us (Ps. 119:115)
- that *God's unfailing love is near us*, even when our world seems to be falling apart (Isaiah 54:10)

To learn more about God's friendship with us, you can read:

- that when we believe God, we can be called His *friend* (James 2:23)
- that Jesus considers us His *friends* because He gave His life for us (John 15:13)
- that when we submit our hearts to obeying God we become His *friends* (John 15:14)

Day 34

We All Need a Little Help

Bible Subject: Christian Fellowship, Prayer, God's Help in Difficult Times

Today's Reading: John 19:25-27, Acts 1:1-14

Today's Verse: "They [all] gathered frequently to pray as a group . . ." (Acts 1:14, Good News Translation)

Today's Lesson: *During a terrible time in her life, Mary met with other believers.*

Wounded animals have a tendency to go off alone and hide, away from the pack or herd, to seek healing in solitude.

When we're wounded and hurting inside, we sometimes have the same tendency. During terrible times in our lives, sometimes the easiest thing to do is to isolate ourselves from other people. Our pain and grief are overwhelming. It's just too hard to talk about what has happened to us, and too painful to be around people who seem to be so happy.

After Jesus' death, no doubt Mary was still hurting terribly. Surely she felt the pull toward isolating herself that's so natural when we're in pain. Yet Mary did the opposite: she sought out the company, or *fellowship,* of other believers, and frequently met with them to pray.

The plan God has for us is to *support* each other in difficult times. As believers, helping one another get through hard times is something we're commanded to do. "Carry one another's burdens," says Galatians 6:2, "and in this way fulfill and observe perfectly the law of Christ" (Amplified Bible). This means that if don't do all we can to help people in their terrible times, we're not living the way God wants us to live. Jesus says in Matthew 25:37 that if we fail to care for people who need help, it's as if we turned our backs on *Him* when He needed help!

God knows that we need each other, *especially* when we're going through terrible times. The Bible tells us that we're supposed to "consider and give attentive, continuous care to watching over one another," looking for ways to encourage and comfort each other [Hebrews 10:24 (Amp.), 1 Thess. 5:11]. This is part of the way God cares for us—to make available to us the loving care of other people who love *Him.*

Prayer: Lord, You are so good to give me friends to help me through hard times. Help me to learn to lean on You and the ones You send to walk with me through life's hard places. And, Lord, show me ways that I can be a helping hand to others in their time of need.

Day 34

For more understanding:

To learn more about God's plan for our relationship with other believers, you can read:

- that we should be *devoted to one another* in love (Rom. 12:10-12)
- that we should *love each other deeply and serve each other* (Galatians 5:13)
- that we should have the attitude that *if one of us suffers, all of us suffer* (1 Cor. 14:26)

To learn more why it's not in God's plan for us to isolate ourselves from other believers, you can read:

- that we're told *not to give up meeting together*, because we need to encourage each other (Heb. 10:25)
- that the early Christians *devoted themselves to fellowship* (Acts 2:42-47)
- that we're told *not to neglect hospitality* to other believers (Heb. 13:2)

To learn more about *how* God wants us to help each other, you can read:

- that we should *pray for one another* (Heb. 13:18, James 5:16)
- that we should *share generously* with those in need and practice *hospitality* (1 Cor. 13:13, Deut. 15:11)
- that we should *share meals and worship together* (Acts 2:42, 45-46)

Naomi

Day 35

Showcasing God

Bible Subject: Joy in the Midst of Sadness, Modeling our Faith

Today's Reading: Ruth 1:1-18

Today's Verse: "My people will be your people and your God my God." Ruth 1:16

Today's Lesson: *Even in a time of sadness and grief, Naomi modeled a faith that drew others to her God.*

Time is a funny thing. You can lose it, you can waste it, it flies when you want it to stand still, and stands still when all you want it to do is pass. Happy times go by in a flash, but when our hearts are full of sadness, each day seems an eternity we can't bear to get through.

For Naomi, the years in Moab must have seemed very long. Since coming to Moab with her family to escape a famine, she'd endured more than ten years of loneliness, grief, and hardship. She'd lost her homeland, her husband, and her sons.

Yet, even though she'd lost so much in her life, Naomi had held on to her God and her faith. And she'd done much more than just hold on. Despite all she'd suffered, Naomi managed to display a faith in her life that inspired her daughter-in-law Ruth to adopt Naomi's God as her own.

When we're walking through times of sadness and grief, it may feel as if we can barely hang on to our own faith, much less model faith to someone else.

How did Naomi do it?

The Bible doesn't tell us. But it *does* tell us what God's answer is to the grief and sorrow in our *own* lives: the joy that we find in His presence (Psalm 16:11). "I will turn their mourning into joy and will comfort them and make them rejoice after their sorrow," God promises in Jeremiah 31:13. As we seek God's presence—in prayer, worship, or simply thinking on Him— He pours such joy into our hearts that it overwhelms our sadness and flows out into our lives. "You have turned my mourning into dancing . . . and [clothed] me with gladness," says Psalm 30:11.

When our lives showcase God's joy despite the pain we're going through, people can't help but notice and be drawn to our God of hope.

Prayer: Dear Lord, Thank You for being the answer for all the hurt places in my life. Thank you for the promise of joy. Help me live in Your presence today.

Day 35

For more understanding:

To learn more about experiencing joy in God's presence, you can read:

- that being in *God's presence* makes us overflow with joy and hope (Romans 15:13)
- that in *God's presence* there is fullness of joy (Psalm 16:11)
- that all creation is joyous in *God's presence* (1 Chronicles 16:33)

To learn more about experiencing joy in the midst of hardship, you can read:

- that Jesus came to give *joy* to those who mourn (Isaiah 61:3)
- that we can be *joyful* in God even though everything is going wrong (Habakkuk 3:17-18)
- that God can turn our crying into *dancing* and our mourning into *joy* (Psalm 30:11)

To learn more about being an example of faith to others, you can read:

- that we're supposed to be the same *example* to others that Christ is to us (1 Peter 2:21)
- that Jesus commands us to follow his *example* of serving others (John 13:15)
- that we're supposed to set an *example* in everything of doing good (Titus 2:7)

Day 36

Lay Down Your Burden

Bible Subject: Grief and Suffering, Faith in Hardship

Today's Reading: Ruth 1

Today's Verses: "Why call me Naomi when the Lord has caused me to suffer and the Almighty has sent such tragedy upon me?" Ruth 1:20-21 (New Living Translation)

"Let us hold firmly to the faith we possess. For we do not have a High Priest who cannot be touched with the feeling of our infirmities . . ." (Hebrews 4:14b-15, NIV and KJV)

Today's Lesson: *Naomi held firmly to her faith even though she was overwhelmed with grief and sorrow.*

Naomi was mired in grief. Yet she must have still believed that God was in control of her life, for she called him God All-Powerful. She was holding tightly to who God is. What she couldn't seem to understand about God is the *why*: Why has her All-Powerful God allowed such suffering in her life?

Naomi's question is one that resonates to us all. Who among us, when tragedy strikes in our lives, has not cried out to God for the answers that Naomi sought? The Psalmist certainly did. "O God my Rock," says Psalm 42:9. "Why have you forgotten me? Why must I wander around in grief?" (New Living Translation).

Even when our faith is strong, when we don't doubt for a moment that God is in control, we can face a challenge when death and grief come calling in our lives. How do we deal with the unimaginable pain of our loss when we know that God has allowed it to happen?

First, we hold tightly to our faith in who God is. Second, we put our hope in His Word (Psalm 130:5)—His Living Word, Jesus Christ (John 1:1). The Bible says that Jesus was "a man of sorrows and acquainted with grief" (Isaiah 53:3, KJV). When we're grieving, we know that Jesus has been where we are. God put Him there, on the cross, to take our suffering upon Himself. Not just so that He would know how we feel—though He does. But so that He could be the *answer* for our suffering, not the why but the *how*.

How do we survive such overwhelming grief? We release the burden to Jesus, and let Him carry it for us. "Surely He has borne our griefs and carried our sorrows," says Isaiah 53:4 (KJV).

Prayer: Oh, Lord, You have done so much for me! Thank You for carrying my griefs and sorrows. I give You all my burdens today and thank You for giving me Your peace.

Day 36

For more understanding:

To learn more about how God comforts us in our grief, you can read:

- that God Himself *comforts* us with His Spirit (Isaiah 51:12, John 14:16-17))
- that Jesus promises that He will not leave us as orphans without *comfort* (John 14:18)
- that God's word *comforts us* and gives us hope (Psalm 119:49-50)

To learn more about how to hold firmly to our faith, you can read

- that we gain full assurance of *faith* when we draw near to God with a sincere heart (Hebrews 10:22)
- that our *faith* increases when we hear the Word of Christ (Romans 10:17)
- that our *faith* increases as we obey God's Word (Luke 17:5-10)

To learn more about putting our hope in God's Word, you can read

- that when we let the *Word* of Christ dwell in us, we also have His peace (Col. 3:15-16)
- that when we put our hope in *God's Word*, we can encourage others (Titus 1:9)
- that when we openly put our hope in *God's Word*, it is a witness to others (Psalm 119:74)

Day 37

Fill Her Up!

Bible Subject: Hoping in God

Today's Reading: Ruth 1, 4:13-17; Job 1-2, 30:16-31, 42:10-17

Today's Verses: "Even if I thought there was still hope for me . . . would you wait until [my sons] grew up? . . . No, my daughters, it is more bitter for me than for you, because the Lord's hand has gone out against me."

"Hope deferred makes the heart sick, but a longing fulfilled is a tree of life." Proverbs

Today's Lesson: *When all her hope was gone, Naomi learned that she could still put her hope in God.*

Naomi was out of hope. Years of difficult circumstances had worn her down, and now her faith was at an all-time low. Her faith was so depleted, she had even begun to think that God had turned against her.

It can happen to the best to us. When hardships keep pounding our faith, year after year, we can get to the place where we feel like every ounce of hope has been pounded out of us. We're so weary of misfortune, we feel like giving up. Like Naomi, we just don't have the strength to keep hoping. Then, when we cry out to God for relief but no relief comes, we may even tell ourselves that God must not be listening. Job felt that way. "I cry out to you O God but you do not answer," complained Job in 30:20.

The Bible tells us differently. First, God is *always* for us, never against us (Romans 8:31). Second, God *always* listens to us, especially when we're suffering. "God has not despised the suffering of the afflicted one . . . but has listened to his cry for help," says Psalm 22:24. No matter how worn out we are from feeling hopeless, God hears us when we cry out to Him—and He has an amazing answer for us: When we hope in the Lord, God changes our hopelessness into strength! "Do you not know? Have you not heard?" says Isaiah 40. "The Lord, the Everlasting God . . . gives strength to the weary and increases the power of the weak . . . Those who hope in [Him] will renew their strength. They will soar on wings like eagles" (vv. 28-29, 31).

And that's not all. God satisfies our longings, too—with Himself. "He satisfies the longing soul, and fills the hungry soul with good," says Psalm 107:9 (Amplified).

How much better can we get than that?

Prayer: Dear Lord, Thank You that you are always for me no matter what my circumstances are! I trust You with my life today. Please give me an extra measure of hope where things seem hopeless. I lean on Your strength today.

Day 37

For more understanding:

To learn more about how God gives us strength, you can read:

- that God's *strength* is made perfect in our weakness (2 Cor. 12:9)
- that God Himself is our *strength* (Habakkuk 3:19)
- that God arms us with *strength* when we need it (Psalm 18:32)

To learn more about how God always listens to us, you can read

- that when we open our griefs to God, He *listens* to us (Psalm 119:26)
- that God *hears* us when we pray (1 John 5:14)
- that God *hears* us when we cry for help (Psalm 31:22)

To learn more about how God satisfies us with Himself, you can read

- that when we seek God He *satisfies* our whole being (Psalm 63:1,5)
- that God *satisfies* us with His goodness (Jeremiah 31:14)
- that God *satisfies* us when we keep our eyes on Him (Psalm 17:15)

Day 38

God's Definition of Love

Bible Subject: Trusting God in Difficult Circumstances, God's Kindness

Today's Reading: Ruth 1-2, 4:9-17

Today's Verse: "My bitterness is much worse than yours because the Lord has sent me so much trouble." Ruth 1:13 (God's Word Translation)

"The Lord bless him, Naomi said . . . 'He has not stopped showing his kindness to the living and the dead.'" Ruth 2:20

Today's Lesson: *Naomi learned to trust in God's kindness, even though she couldn't make sense of the trouble He had allowed in her life.*

Some people have much more hardship in their lives than others do. It just doesn't seem fair, does it? Especially when it happens to *us*. The idea that life *should* be fair, but isn't, seems to be gnawing at Naomi's heart—and her faith.

When bad things keep happening to us, over and over again, our faith can take a beating. We, like Naomi, may begin to feel like we're all alone, drowning in a sea of trouble. And God seems to be nowhere in sight.

If we can't see God because of all our troubles, we need to start looking in a different direction: away from our difficult circumstances, and toward the face of our God. "Look to the Lord," says Psalm 105:4. "Seek His face always." When we focus on our circumstances, we miss what God wants to show us—"the incomparable riches of His grace, expressed in His kindness in Christ Jesus" (Ephesians 2:7).

God's kindness. That's what Naomi saw when she finally stopped looking at her circumstances, and started looking at God character.* The Bible says that God loves us with "everlasting kindness" (Isaiah 54:8). The greatest way God has shown His kindness to us is that "while we were yet sinners, Christ died for us" (Romans 5:8). That means that Jesus is God's definition of love (Ephesians 2:4)!

No matter how much hardship we find in our lives, we can always find God's love in the midst. "'Though the mountains be shaken, and the hills be removed, yet my unfailing love for you will not be shaken,' says the Lord" (Isaiah 54:10). The Bible promises that *nothing* can separate us from the love of Christ, *especially* not our circumstances (Romans 8:35).

When we keep our eyes on Jesus, instead of seeing the waves of trouble around us, all we see is His face—and His love.

Prayer: Dear Lord, how great is Your love and kindness! Help me to see Your kindness today no matter what I am dealing with.

---

*In v. 2:20 Naomi seems to be acknowledging that kindness is an essential part of God's character, since she asks God to bless *Boaz* for *his* kindness to Ruth.

Day 38

For more understanding:

To learn more about God's kindness, you can read:

- that God is gracious and compassionate and abounding in *kindness* (Joel 2:13, NIV and KJV)
- that God's merciful *kindness* is our comfort (Psalm 119:76)
- that God shows us His wonderful *kindness* by helping us when our circumstances make us feel like we're under attack (Psalm 31:21, Amplified)

To learn more about finding God's love in the midst of hardship, you can read:

- that *God's perfect love* for us drives out all fear (1 John 4:18)
- that *God's love* gives us perseverance through hardship (2 Thess. 3:5)
- that no trouble or hardship can separate us from the *love of Christ* (Romans 8:35)

To learn more about how to keep our eyes on God, you can read

- that we *keep our eyes on God* by seeking His presence (Psalm 17:15, Amp.)
- that we must *look to God* to help us instead of focusing on our troubles (Psalm 121)
- that we *keep our eyes on God* by remembering that our only true help comes from Him (Psalm 25:15)

Day 39

Sit Still, Please!

Bible Subject: Hope, Waiting on God

Today's Reading: Ruth 1:1-18, 3-4

Today's Verses: "Don't call me Naomi (Pleasant). Call me Marah (bitter) . . . I had everything I wanted when I left but now the Lord brings me home with nothing." Ruth 1:21 (Easy-to-read Version)

"Wait, my daughter, until you find out what happens." Ruth 3:18

"Sit still, my daughter, until you know how the matter will fall." Ruth 3:18, KJV

Today's Lesson: *Naomi learned to wait on God for the good things He had planned for her life.*

Little boys are by nature the most wiggly of creatures. They can't seem to sit still for a minute . . . literally. Ask any first grade teacher.

Being still is hard for us believers, too—when it means waiting on God to do something in our lives that we desperately want Him to do.

Naomi's life had been full of every good thing she'd ever wanted. Then she experienced tragedy, and suddenly it was all gone. And so, it seems, was Naomi's faith.

Who can blame her? Faith is easy when everything is going well in our lives. But when the going gets tough . . . well, having faith gets tough too. When we're in the midst of long periods of hardship, it can seem like nothing in our life will ever be good again.

When our hope for good begins to grow thin, it's time to put our hope in God alone, and trust in *His* goodness. Then comes the really hard part: sitting still, waiting for God's goodness to unfold. As we wait on God, we learn to know His character. "Be still and know that I am God," says Psalm 46:10. While we're in that waiting mode, with our hearts still and open to God's Spirit, we can feel God's presence and hear His voice more clearly. The Bible calls this *seeking God*. When we seek God, He fills us with His own goodness (Psalm 107:9)—and His hope. "The Lord is good to those whose hope is in Him, to the one who seeks Him," says Lamentations 3:25.

God lays out His plans for our good in Jeremiah 29:11, "plans to prosper you and not to harm you, plans to give you hope and a future." What God has in store for us is always the very best that could happen to us (Romans 8:28).

God's plans for us are worth waiting for!

Prayer: Oh, Lord, help me to seek You today with all my heart. Thank You for Your good plans for my life this day. Give me the grace to wait while You are working out the details.

Day 39

For more understanding:

To learn more about God's goodness, you can read

- that every purpose of God is part of His *goodness* (2 Thess. 1:11)
- that the earth is full of God's *goodness* (Psalm 33:5, KJV)
- that God stores up His *goodness* for us (Psalm 31:19)

To learn more about God's plans for our good, you can read

- that God brings to completion every *good work* that He begins in our lives (Phil. 1:6)
- that every *good and perfect thing* in our life is a gift from God (James 1:17)
- that God promises not to withhold any *good thing* from His people (Psalm 84:11)

To learn more about seeking God, you can read:

- that we *seek God* by calling upon Him (Isaiah 55:6)
- that we *seek God* by believing that He exists and that He rewards those who desire Him (Hebrews 11:6)
- that we *seek God* by asking for His presence in our lives (Luke 11:10)

Day 40

Life at the Top

Bible Subject: Redemption, Hope, Abundant Life

Today's Reading: Ruth 1-4

Today's Verse: "Praise be to the Lord, who has not left you this day without a kinsman-redeemer . . . He will renew your life and sustain you in your old age." Ruth 4:11

Today's Lesson: *Naomi learned that God could renew her life and change her despair into hope.*

To kids of the 1950's and '60's, few things provoked more excitement than redeeming trading stamps for fun stuff from catalogs. Today's kids feel the same tingly anticipation scrolling through Amazon to cash in a gift card for a new movie or toy. Either way, the kid comes out on top—getting something new and exciting in exchange for something that doesn't have much value unless you trade it in.

Naomi had suffered years of hardship that had brought her to the brink of despair and made her feel that her life had little value. Then she learned an amazing thing about God: He will never leave us without a way to *redeem*, or trade in, our lives devoid of hope for new and transformed lives in Him. The Bible tells us that "it was not with perishable things such as silver and gold that you were redeemed from the empty way of life handed down to you from your forefathers, but with the precious blood of Christ . . . so your faith and hope are in God" (1 Peter 1:18-19).

Jesus' act of redemption on the cross gives our lives great value that they didn't have before. In Christ, we can "trade in" our empty lives of despair for new lives full of hope. That's why Jesus came: "to bring good tidings to the . . . afflicted . . . to heal the broken-hearted . . . to comfort all who mourn . . . and to grant them consolation and joy . . . instead of a heavy, burdened spirit" (Isaiah 61:1-3, Amplified). Our only part in the trade is that we must believe in Him and open our hearts to receive Him (John 1:12). Then He gives us a brand new life—the best that we could ever have. "I came that they might have life and have it to the full," Jesus said in John 10:10.

What a deal! With Christ in our lives, we always come out on top!

Prayer: Lord, I praise You today for the full and abundant life You give. Thank You for redeeming my life! I open my heart to You today and receive Your healing, comfort and joy.

Day 40

For more understanding:

To learn more about how God can redeem our lives, you can read:

- that through Christ *our lives are redeemed* from the power of death (1 Cor. 15:55-57)
- that God *redeems our life* from destruction and covers us with love (Psalm 103:4, KJV)
- that God *redeems our life* by judging in our favor (Lamentations 3:58)

To learn more about the abundant life we have in Christ, you can read

- that in Jesus we have *life,* and that *life* is the light of the world (John 1:4)
- that there is *true life* and great spiritual treasure when we take hold of Christ (1 Tim. 6:19)
- that God's *abundant grace governs our lives* when we belong to Christ (Rom. 5:17)

To learn more about how our lives are empty without God, you can read

- that our *lives without God* are fleeting and like a phantom (Psalm 39:4-6)
- that *our lives without God* are hopeless (Epehsians 2:12)
- that *without God in our lives* we are weak and powerless (Romans 5:6)

Martha of Bethany

Day 41

Service, Please

Bible Subject: Service

Today's Reading: Luke 10:38-42, Revelation 3:14-22

Today's Verse: "[Jesus] came to a village where a woman named Martha opened her home to Him." Luke 10:38

Today's Lesson: *Martha showed her love for God by serving others.*

Home is where the heart is. When we think of home, we get all warm and fuzzy inside. Lighted windows come to mind, people we love, being safe, warm, and comfortable. To most of us, home is much more than just a *place.* It's at the very center of the meaning of *love.*

That's why Martha opening her home to Jesus was so significant. Far more than just an invitation to share a meal, Martha's open door to her *home* symbolizes an open door to her *heart* as well.

Jesus Himself compares the two in Revelation 3:20, when He says, "I stand at the door and knock. If anyone hears my voice and opens the door, I will come in and eat with him . . ." Here Jesus isn't talking about sharing a meal, or even asking people to make a decision to follow Him. He's talking about a condition of heart among people who already consider themselves believers, but whose deeds demonstrate that their hearts are really closed to the full extent of His love. 'If you really love me,' Jesus is saying, 'show it—by opening your heart wide enough to let me come in and influence your life, so that your deeds will reflect my love.'

It's not enough just to *say* we love God. We show our love for God by what we *do*.

When Martha opened her front door to Jesus, she had a purpose: to show Him her love by serving him a meal. We too can show our love for God by *our* acts of service to others. How? The Bible tells us: let every act of service flow out of love. "Let your love be sincere . . . never lag in zeal and earnest endeavor . . . Be aglow and burning with the Spirit, serving the Lord" (Romans 12:11).

You want to serve Jesus, like Martha did? Then serve other people!

Prayer: Lord God, Thank You for coming into my life and showing me Your great love. Help me serve others today in Your name.

Day 41

For more understanding:

To learn more about how to show our love for God, you can read:

- that we *show our love for God* by being merciful to others (Jude 21)
- that we *show our love for God* by having an attitude of love toward other believers (1 Thess. 4:9)
- that we *show our love for God* by having an attitude of love toward people who act hatefully toward us (Luke 6:35)

To learn more about opening our hearts to God's love, you can read

- that we *open our hearts to God* by letting Him rule as Lord in our lives (1 Peter 3:15)
- that we *open our hearts to God* by removing anything from our lives that keeps us from putting Him first (2 Chronicles 20:33)
- that Jesus's love *lives in our hearts* when we have faith in him (Ephesians 3:15)

To learn more about how our acts of service honor God, you can read

- that *acts of service honor God* when they come from faith (Phil 2:17)
- that *acts of service honor God* when they're accompanied by love, faith, and patient endurance of hardship (Rev. 2:19)
- that *acts of service honor God* when we serve readily and cheerfully (Ephesians. 6:7)

Day 42

A Spiritual Heart-Check

Bible Subject: Serving God, Listening to God

Today's Reading: Luke 10:38-42, John 13:1-17

Today's Verses: "But Martha was cumbered about much serving." (Luke 10:40, KJV)

"Jesus showed [His disciples] the full extent of His love [when He washed their feet]." John 13:1

Today's Lesson: *Martha learned that she needed to listen to God to determine the way that He wanted her to serve Him.*

Doctors recommend that we all have regular heart checks*. Sometimes we need spiritual heart checks, too.

Each of us has a different "calling" on our life, different work that God wants us to do to serve Him (1 Cor. 12:5-6). Martha's way of serving God was hospitality. But she was going about it all wrong. She didn't have the right attitude of heart. She needed a heart check, and

Jesus told her the way she could get it was to spend time listening to Him *first* (see v. 42).

We can learn from Martha about the right way to serve our God. We should always seek God *first* to make sure what we're doing is what *He* wants us to do. The Bible says that God "calls" us according to the purpose He has for each of our lives (Romans 8:28). This means that He speaks to our hearts to tell us what He wants us to do. How can we hear Him speak to us if we're not listening?

Once we know *what* we're supposed to do, our listening to God is not finished; it's only begun. In His Word, God tells us repeatedly that true service to Him requires the right condition of heart: a loving spirit. "Serve one another in love," says Galatians 5:13. When we do this, we're following the example Jesus Himself set for us (John 13:1-17).

We should never let serving *cumber* us, as it did Martha, becoming nothing more than a burdensome chore. Instead, the Bible tells us that serving the Lord should be joyful! "Serve the Lord with gladness; come before His presence with singing," proclaims Psalm 100:2 (KJV). The right way to serve the Lord is with hearts overflowing with love and joy. And how do our hearts get that way? By coming into God's presence so that we can know Him better.

Prayer: Dear Lord, I seek You first today! I desire to know Your purpose and call for my life and to walk in that today. Let Your love overflow into my heart to all I meet.

---

*http://www.heart.org/HEARTORG/Conditions/Heart-Health-Screenings

Day 42

For more understanding:

To learn more about hearing God's voice in our hearts, you can read:

- that hardening our hearts against God (ignoring Him) can keep us from hearing *God's voice* (Hebrews 3:7-14)
- that most important part of *listening to God* is doing what He tells you (Romans 3:13)
- that God rewards us when we listen to *His voice* (Psalm 81:11-16)

To learn more about having the right condition of heart, you can read,

- that waiting for the Lord gives us *strength of heart* (Psalm 27:14)
- that having a *heart devoted totally to God* gives us clear spiritual vision (Matt. 5:8)
- that having *a right heart* gives us a desire to please God (Ephesians 6:6)

To learn more about how to get the joy of the Lord in our lives, you can read

- that making God's Word a part of our lives brings us *joy* (Isaiah 61:10-11)
- that praising God brings us *joy* (Psalm 149)
- that being in God's presence brings *exceeding joy* (Jude 24, KJV)

Day 43

Hold On Tight!

Bible Subject: Our Relationship with God, Idols in our Lives

Today's Reading: Luke 10:38-42

Today's Verses: "Martha, overly occupied and too busy, was distracted with much serving." (Luke 10:40, Amplified)

"Take diligent heed to hold fast to [God] and to serve Him with all your heart, and your very life." (Joshua 22:5, NIV and Amplified)

Today's Lesson: *Martha learned that she needed be careful not to let anything interfere with her relationship with God.*

Today's women are busy. We have families to care for, jobs to go to, classes to attend, chores to do, kids and groceries to load into the car, and miles to drive before we sleep. On top of that, we're supposed to stay fit, beautiful, and sane.

How do we find time for it all? How do we find time for God in the *midst* of it all?

ELIZABETH McDAVID JONES

Martha had the same problem. She was so busy trying to *serve* Jesus, she had stopped *listening* to Him, and she didn't even realize it. Martha had allowed herself to be *too* busy . . . period. Even if what she was busy doing was something good—serving others— it had distracted her from what was *best*, spending time with Jesus.

With lives that are so busy, it's easy to let our time with God slip— until it's gone entirely. The Bible tells us to take *diligent heed* to hold fast to God (Joshua 22:5). That means that we should pay close attention to our relationship with God and constantly be on guard against *anything* that interferes. "Above all else, guard your heart," we're told in Proverbs 4:23. The Bible calls things that we love more than God "idols." Idols can be money, jobs, possessions, politics, even relationships—anything that takes us away from God.

Being close to God is the most important thing we can spend our time doing. In fact, it's the very reason God created us (Isaiah 43:7, Col. 1:16)! God doesn't want a half-hearted relationship with us. He wants us to hold on to him for dear life, because that's the way He holds on to us! The Bible says that wherever we go or whatever we do, "God's right hand holds us fast" (Psalm 139:10).

Prayer: Oh, Lord, forgive me for being too busy for You so much of the time. Help me keep You first over all things in my life. Please order my life today so that I have time to do all You call me to this day.

Day 43

For more understanding:

To learn more about paying careful attention to our relationship with God, you can read:

- that we receive a blessing when we *concentrate on our relationship with God* (Luke 12:37)
- that God rewards us when we *diligently* seek *a relationship with Him* (Hebrew 11:6)
- that Jesus wants our relationship with Him to be *passionate and burning with zeal*, not half-hearted or lukewarm (Rev. 3:16, 19)

To learn more about idols in our lives, you can read:

- that *anything we treasure more than God* is an idol and all idols are worthless compared to God (Isaiah 9:6)
- that *when we make our own interests and desires more important than God*, we're serving idols (Colossians 3:5, Amplified)
- that *anything we desire too much* can become an idol (1 Cor. 10:6-7)

To learn more about how to guard our hearts and minds against spiritual idolatry, you can read:

- that we must *turn our minds toward God* and away from earthly pleasures (Col. 3:5)
- that the *understanding we get from God* gives us the ability to keep ourselves from serving idols (1 John 5:20-21)
- that *honoring God as first in our lives* keeps us from idolatry (Leviticus 19:4)

Day 44

Listen Up!

Bible Subject: God's Presence, Listening to God

Today's Reading: Luke 10:38-41

Today's Verse: "Martha, Martha, you are worried and upset about many things, but only one thing is needed." (Luke 10:41-42)

Today's Lesson: *Martha learned that the only way she could have a satisfying relationship with God was to spend time in His presence listening to Him.*

Satisfaction guaranteed! Words like that make us sit up and listen—and probably buy something we don't really need. Because who doesn't want to be satisfied? Especially when it comes to relationships.

Martha was no different. She was trying hard to have a satisfying relationship with Jesus—too hard, it seems. She was busily serving Jesus, striving to please Him and win His favor. The result: she ended up worried and upset. And still no closer to the kind of relationship with Jesus that she wanted.

What was she doing wrong?

It certainly wasn't lack of effort. Martha was making an *extreme* effort. Problem was, her efforts were in the wrong direction. Because she was doing what *she* thought she needed to do, instead of listening to Jesus, her efforts were taking her farther away from Jesus instead of closer. She wasn't doing the "one thing" that Jesus said was needed: sitting at His feet, listening to Him.

The Bible tells us that in God's presence we'll be "abundantly satisfied" (Psalm 36:8). Spending time with Him is the *only* way to have the relationship with Him that He desires to have with us (Psalm 104:13). What should we do while we're there? Listen— and then obey what we hear, or "walk," as the Bible sometimes calls obedience. Psalm 143:8 says, "Cause me to hear your loving-kindness in the morning, for on you do I lean and put my trust. Cause me to know the way wherein I should walk, for I lift up my inner self to you" (Amplified). Amazing! When we stop striving and start listening to God, we can actually hear his lovingkindness! With such a beautiful sound in our ears, how can we go wrong?

And when we start our day off by listening to God, the Bible promises that we will know the right way to walk . . . straight to His presence.

Prayer: Lord, I want to LIVE in Your presence. You are the most important thing in my life. Help me hear Your lovingkindness to me today.

Day 44

For more understanding:

To learn more about how to find satisfaction in life, you can read:

- that listening to God *satisfies us* more than anything else can (Isaiah 55:1-2)
- that God's love *satisfies us* (Psalm 107:8-9, Psalm 90:14)
- that God alone provides everything we need to *satisfy us* (Isaiah 58:11)

To learn more about hearing God and obeying Him, you can read:

- that faith comes from *hearing the Word of God and obeying it* (Romans 10:17-21)
- that we're supposed to be active *doers of the Word, not merely listeners* (James 1:22)
- that we receive a blessing when we *hear God's Word and do what it says* (James 1:25, Amplified)

To learn more about our relationship with God, you can read:

- that our *relationship with Jesus* depends upon our submitting our lives to Jesus in response to His Word (Rev. 3:20)
- that having a *relationship with God* enables us to hear His voice (John 8:47)
- that our *relationship with God* depends upon us earnestly and diligently seeking Him (Hebrews 11:6, Amplified)

Day 45

Dress-Up Time

Bible Subject: Seeking God during Terrible Times, God's Presence

Today's Reading: John 11:1-45

Today's Verse: "When Martha heard that Jesus was coming, she went out to meet Him." John 11:20

Today's Lesson: *In a terrible time in her life, Martha turned to Jesus.*

Martha's brother Lazarus had died. Most likely he was her "baby" brother, too, and still a very young man.* Martha must have been devastated—too devastated to even think of serving all the company gathered at her house. What Martha *did* do was seek Jesus. When she heard he was near, she left the guests behind and rushed to meet Him. Martha poured out her sorrow to Jesus, and Jesus met her needs—with faith (v. 40). "Did I not tell you that if you believed, you would see the glory of God?" Jesus asked. As we exercise faith, we're able to see and experience God's glory—His character. The Bible promises that God's glory is a "rich treasury" of strength when we need it (Ephesians 3:16).

In the darkest times of our lives, we desperately need God's strength, because we have none of our own. When we seek God's presence, Ephesians 3:16 tells us that we're "reinforced" with the power of God's own Spirit (Amplified). "Incline your ear and come to Me," says Isaiah 55:3, "and your soul will revive." God's presence is medicine for our soul!

But there's more. When we're hurting so much we don't feel like going anywhere or doing anything, God gives us beautiful spiritual clothes to dress up in: "a [crown] of beauty instead of ashes**, the [perfume] of joy instead of mourning, and a garment of praise instead of a heavy, burdened, and failing spirit" (Isaiah 61:3, Amplified). All we have to do is what Martha did: seek God's presence.

Martha rushed out to meet Jesus on the road, but we can meet Him wherever we are. "I am with you always," Jesus says in Matthew 28:20, "even until the end of [time]."

Prayer: Lord Jesus, how I thank You and praise You that You are my comfort when I grieve. Thank You for being an ever-present help for me. Help me today to know Your presence as I go about this day.

---

*In Bible times, men were always the head of the household. Since Lazarus was apparently living with his sister Martha, it stands to reason that he probably had not yet reached the age of majority.

**In Bible times, people heaped ashes on their heads to show they were in mourning.

Day 45

For more understanding:

To learn more about how to seek God, you can read:

- that we *seek God* by learning His Word (Psalm 119:10-11)
- that we *seek God* by living our lives the way He tells us to in His Word (Ps. 119:2,7)
- that we *seek God* whenever we spend time in His Presence praying or praising Him (Ps. 119:2,7; 2 Chronicles 7:14)

To learn more about how God seeks us, you can read:

- that *Jesus came to seek us* and bring us to salvation (Luke 19:9-10)
- that God wants to have a relationship with us so much that *He seeks us* before we even seek Him (Isaiah 65:1-3, Romans 10:20)
- that God is actively seeking people who want to worship Him sincerely (John 4:23)

To learn more about how God helps us in terrible times, you can read:

- that *God's word strengthens us* when we're weary with sorrow (Psalm 119:28)
- that *Jesus promises to comfort us* when we're in mourning (Matt. 5:4)
- that *God's Spirit comes to comfort us* and give us peace when we're troubled (John 14:26-27)

Day 46

Prove It!

Bible Subject: Faith, Waiting on God, Trusting in God's Character

Today's Reading: John 11:1-46

Today's Verses: "Then Martha, as soon as she heard that Jesus was coming, went and met Him but Mary sat still in the house." John 11:20 (KJV)

"Jesus said to [Martha], 'I am Myself the Resurrection and the Life . . . Do you believe this?'" John 11:25-26 (Amplified)

Today's Lesson: *Martha learned that waiting on God is an important component of faith.*

Impulses are powerful motivators. American retailers count on it, don't they? Especially with us women. Why else do they put the most expensive handbags and shoes on the busiest department store aisles?

Martha was a woman who always seemed to act on impulse. When she heard that Jesus was coming to the funeral for her brother Lazarus, Martha couldn't *wait* to show Jesus her faith. She rushed out to meet

Him on the road, proclaiming that she knew Jesus could have healed her brother, if only He'd come a little sooner. But instead of congratulating Martha for her *great* faith, Jesus seems to question whether she has *enough* faith (vv. 25-26). And He *doesn't* question her sister Mary's faith, when Mary says the same thing to Him later (v. 32).

What's the difference? Could it be that Mary's willingness to wait patiently for Jesus to come to her showed more faith than Martha's impulsive rush to meet Him?

The Bible says that our deeds prove our faith (James 2:18). Believe it or not, sitting still can be a deed—when it focuses us on who God is. "Be still and know that I am God," says Psalm 46:10. Perhaps this was Martha's problem: maybe she acted so impulsively because she was focused only on what Jesus *could* do but *hadn't* done (heal her brother), instead of who He was, the very Author of life itself!

It takes a lot more faith to sit still, waiting for God to take action Himself, than it does for us to rush out on impulse and do something to try to help Him out.

Waiting on God means trusting in who God is, even though we can't see or understand what He's doing. That's what faith is: "the assurance of things that we [can only] hope for, and the proof of things that we cannot see" (Hebrews 11:1, Amplified).

Prayer: Oh, Lord Jesus, You are so faithful. Teach me to wait patiently as You work in my life.

Day 46

For more understanding:

To learn more about faith, you can read:

- that we must let our lives be controlled by *faith* in our God, not by what we can or cannot see in the natural realm (2 Cor. 5:7)
- that when we live by *faith*, God upholds us and gives us success (2 Chron. 20:2)
- that having *faith* is essential to an effective prayer life (Mark 11:22-25)

To learn more about trusting God, you can read

- that we should put our *trust in the power of God* rather than in worldly power (Psalm 20:2)
- that the more we *trust God*, the less fear can control our life (Psalm 56:4)
- that when we *trust in God*, we'll never be put to shame (Romans 9:33)

To learn more about sitting still in the spirit, you can read

- that we're all commanded to *be still* in God's presence (Zechariah 2:13)
- that we should *be still* and consider God's wonders (Job 37:14)
- that even God sometimes holds himself back in *stillness* (Isaiah 42:14)

Day 47

Ow-ies from God

Bible Subject: God's Discipline

Today's Reading: Luke 10:38-42; John 11:1-43

Today's Verses: "Now Jesus loved Martha and her sister and Lazarus. They were His dear friends and He held them in loving esteem." (John 11:5, Amplified)

"Martha, Martha, you are worried and upset about many things, but only one thing is needed. Mary has chosen what is better, and it will not be taken away from her." Luke 10:41-42

Today's Lesson: *Martha could bear the pain of Jesus' reprimands because she knew how much He loved her.*

Growing up as the oldest sibling isn't all it's cracked up to be. Sure, you may get privileges that your younger brothers and sisters don't, like having your own room or staying up later, but you're always expected to set a good example for the younger ones. Sometimes you wish you could magically escape and be the youngest for a change. Martha may have wished that, too. Especially when Jesus told her she needed to follow the example of her *younger* sister Mary. Ouch!

Jesus' reprimand must have hurt Martha deeply. Why doesn't the Bible show us her pain? Maybe it's because we're meant to look instead at the extent of Jesus' love for her, and to realize that it was out of love that Jesus *gave* her the rebuke.

God's rebukes to us work the same way. Knowing how much we're loved helps us receive God's discipline in the right spirit. Christ's love for us is so "wide and long and high and deep" that we can't even understand it (Ephesians 3:19) And in Revelation 3:19, Jesus reminds a church—and us— that "those whom I dearly and tenderly love, I tell their faults and convict and convince and reprove and chasten. I discipline [them] and instruct [them]" (Amplified Bible).

That doesn't mean it's easy to receive God's discipline in our lives. It hurts!

Yet Martha undoubtedly knew—and we should remember—that God's discipline is not a punishment, but a learning opportunity. Because God loves us so much, He wants us to learn how to please Him. The Bible tells us that God disciplines us for "our certain good" so that we can "share in His holiness" and participate in His purposes (Hebrews 12:10).

Like a loving parent, God trains us so that we can become the very best that we can be!

Prayer: Father God, thank You for being such a loving Father to me! Help me learn and grow from Your discipline. Open my eyes to see the learning opportunities You have prepared for me today.

Day 47

For more understanding:

To learn more about God's discipline, you can read:

- that we should consider *God's discipline* to be a blessing because it means God is teaching us (Psalm 94:12)
- that *God's discipline* is a sign of His love for us (Proverbs 3:12)
- that *God's discipline* is a sign that we are His children (Deut. 8:5)

To learn more about how much God loves us, you can read

- that every single thing God does is a result of *His love* (Psalm 25:10)
- that *God loves* us so much He took the punishment for our sins upon Himself (John 3:16)
- that *God's love* for us is so great it's beyond our understanding (Ephesians 3:19)

To learn more about how God is like a parent to us, you can read

- that God promises to comfort us *like a mother* comforts her child (Isaiah 66:13)
- that God's love for us is so great He calls us *His own children* (1 John 3:1)
- that God is a *father* to the fatherless (Psalm 68:5)

Day 48

God's Test-Taking

Bible Subject: Faith

Today's Reading: John 11:1-29, Hebrews 11:17-19, Genesis 22:1-10

Today's Verses: "Did I not tell you that if you believed, you would see the glory of God?" (John 11:40)

"By faith Abraham, while the testing of his faith was still in progress, had already brought Isaac for an offering . . ." (Hebrews 11:17, Amplified Bible)

Today's Lesson: *Martha learned that Jesus tested her faith so that she could grow in faith.*

We're a society obsessed with test-taking. We test infants moments after they're born, and the testing goes on endlessly throughout their lives: at school, in the workplace, in the doctor's office, everywhere. We're constantly graded, cataloged, processed, and diagnosed according to test results. Why? So that people who want to know about us can gather information . . . in the name of helping us, of course.

God gives us tests, too—faith tests. But His tests aren't meant to gather information on us, since God knows everything about us before we're even born (Jeremiah 1:5). Rather, God gives us faith tests so that we can learn about ourselves—and about Him. The Bible says that growing in faith is learning not to trust our senses but instead to trust *God* (Hebrews 11:1, Amplified). Testing our faith is one way God disciplines and instructs us. It's a trial and error process, through which we gradually build more and more faith.

Take Martha, for instance. Seems she was constantly getting upstaged in the faith department by her sister Mary (also see Luke 10:38-41). Jesus questioned Martha's faith yet again after her brother Lazarus had died. Martha's answer to Jesus showed that her faith had its limits. She believed in a resurrection for all believers *someday,* but she couldn't seem to wrap her mind around the idea that Jesus was talking about raising her brother from the dead *today.* Jesus kept trying to get Martha to understand that our faith needn't be dependent on what we can see or even what we can imagine.

Most of us have the same faith problem that Martha had. We continually limit the way God can work in our lives because we have so little faith. But God is faithful even when we aren't. He keeps giving us faith tests until we pass them with flying colors.

God never gives up on us!

Prayer: Lord Jesus, Thank you so very much that You never give up on me. Sometimes my faith is so small, even after I have seen You work great things in my life. I believe You; please help my unbelief today!

Day 48

For more understanding:

To learn more about how God tests our faith, you can read:

- that God uses His Word *to test the thoughts and attitudes of our hearts* (Heb. 4:12)
- that God allows trials in our lives *to test the genuineness of our faith* (1 Peter 1:7, 4:12)
- that God *tests our faith* so that we will learn to call on Him (Zechariah 13:9)

To learn more about how we grow in faith, you can read

- that God allows trials into our lives so that our *faith can grow* (Acts 14:22, 1 Peter 1:7)
- that our *faith grows* by exercising our faith (Luke 17:5-6)
- that our *faith grows* by hearing and obeying God's Word (Romans 10:17)

To learn more about the ways God teaches us, you can read

- that *God teaches* us by making us aware of whether or not our thoughts honor Him (Psalm 139:23, Philippians 4:8)
- that *God teaches* us through His Word (Psalm 119:66)
- that *God's Spirit teaches* us about spiritual truths (1 Corinthians 2:13)

Day 49

Spiritual Shopping Spree

Bible Subject: Serving God

Today's Reading: John 12:1-11

Today's Verses: "Martha served." John 12:2

"Well done, thou good and faithful servant." Matthew 25:21, KJV

Today's Lesson: *Martha served God at every opportunity.*

Calling all shoppers! How'd you like to go on a shopping spree—grab everything off the shelf that strikes your fancy, rush to the checkout, and have someone else pay for it all? Sound like a dream come true?

Guess what? We *can* go on a shopping spree—a spiritual one. And the Bible tells us we should. "Buy up every opportunity," says Ephesians 5:16, "because the days are evil." Colossians 4:5 takes it a step further. We're told to "seize the opportunity," making the very most of our time (Amplified Bible). Imagine. We're not just supposed to shop (spiritually); we're supposed to buy everything in sight—every opportunity, that is. That's what Martha did. Wherever God put her, she seized the opportunity to serve.

We can do the same. How? Colossians tells us: "Be wise in the way you act toward non-Christians, living prudently and with discretion (4:5, Amplified)." In other words, we're not supposed to take every opportunity to *tell* unbelievers what they're doing *wrong*. We're supposed to *show* them what's right by the way we live our lives! Ephesians 5:9 (Amplified Bible) gives us specifics. Our lives should show "every form of kindly goodness, uprightness of heart, and trueness of life." We serve the Lord where He puts us, living lives full of love and good deeds towards whomever He brings across our path (v. 11).

We need to do what Martha did: seize every opportunity God gives us! We must look around with spiritual eyes wide open, to see what opportunities to serve others God has put upon our life's shelves, and then hurry to buy them up. That's how we can be faithful servants who will please God (Matthew 25:21).

Let's go on a spiritual shopping spree today!

Prayer: Dear Lord, I ask for Your help as I go about my day. Help me see the opportunities You are giving me to serve and help others to know You.

Day 49

For more understanding:

To learn more about seizing opportunities to serve God, you can read:

- that we're supposed to *seize opportunities* to do good to all people, especially other believers (Galatians 6:10)
- that we must *seize the critical opportunity* God has placed before us to live lives that look like Jesus rather than the world (Romans 13:11-14, Amplified)
- that we must keep a sense of urgency and *seize every opportunity* to share God's Word with others (2 Tim. 4:2, Amplified)

To learn more about showing people what's right with the example of our lives, you can read

- that our lives are supposed to be *constant proofs* of what's acceptable to God (Ephesians 5:10)
- that Jesus purposely sets us an *example* that we're supposed to follow (John 13:15)
- that it is *commendable before God* for us to suffer for doing good (1 Peter 2:21)

To learn more about being faithful servants, you can read

- that Jesus humbled Himself and made Himself a *servant* for our sake (Phil. 2:7)
- that *our faithfulness as servants* is measured by whether we actually do what we know God expects us to do (Luke 12:43)
- that we're faithful servants when we conform wholly to Christ's example in living (John 12:26)

Mary of Bethany

Day 50

Stray Sheep

Bible Subject: Listening to God, Living the Christian Life

Today's Reading: Luke 10:38-41

Today's Verses: "[Mary] sat at the Lord's feet listening to what He said . . . But Martha came to Jesus and asked, Lord, don't you care that my sister has left me to do the work myself? Tell her to help me!" Luke 10:39-40

"Mary has chosen what is better . . ." Luke 10:42

Today's Lesson: *Mary listened to Jesus, even though it went against what her culture expected her to do.*

Human beings are herd animals. No wonder the Bible compares us to sheep! "All we like sheep have gone astray," says the prophet Isaiah (53:6). Yes, we're followers by nature—crowd-pleasers. We crave that feeling of acceptance, of fitting in. No one wants to be the odd-man-out, the outsider looking in. It's why we're so prone to bend to peer pressure and to give in to societal norms that we may not even agree with. Most of us get our feelings of self-worth from pleasing the people in our lives who matter to us.

When Mary chose to sit at Jesus' feet rather than help her older sister Martha prepare a meal for Jesus, she was "bucking against" the expectations of her culture. Hospitality was all-important in Bible times, as was honoring your elders. A family's reputation was at stake whenever they entertained guests, and going against the wishes of the head of the family, as Martha obviously was, was considered a family disgrace. Therefore, what Mary did was unthinkable in her culture. How hard it must have been for Mary to resist such social pressure in order to listen to Jesus!

It's the same for us today. What the Bible tells us to do is often at odds with what society expects us to do. The Bible calls it "foolish" to follow other people rather than listen to Jesus. Instead, we're supposed to "live purposefully, worthily, and accurately" (Ephesians 5:15, Amplified).

If there's an *accurate* way to live, that means there's an *inaccurate* way also. There's a choice to be made about how we live our lives—the way of the world, or God's way. Jesus was emphatic that Mary made the right choice. Will we?

Prayer: Lord Jesus, I want to sit at Your feet today. I want to choose the right thing as I go about this day. Help me to know what that is, and to obey, even when I do not meet the expectations of others.

Day 50

For more understanding:

To learn more about following God's expectations rather than the world's expectations, you can read:

- that we should not fashion ourselves according to the world's customs but *allow Christ to transform our minds* and give us new ideals and attitudes (Romans 12:12a, Amplified)
- that we must be on guard against *following human traditions* and the principles of this world *rather than Christ* (Col. 2:8)
- that we cannot honor God with worship that is *based on human tradition rather than on sincere hearts dedicated to Him* (Isaiah 29:13)

To learn more about how to understand what God's will for us is, you can read

- that, as we allow Christ to transform our minds, we gain greater understanding of *God's will* (Romans 12:12b)
- that it is *God's will* for us to live good and honest lives that are a positive example for others (1 Peter 2:15, Amplified)
- that, when we submit to God's Spirit, He helps us carry out *His will* in our lives (Hebrew 13:21)

To learn more about living the way God wants us to live, you can read

- that God wants us to *behave graciously* toward non-believers, so that we can win them to the Lord (Colossians 4:5)
- that that we must clothe ourselves with Christ by *living lives that look different* from the lives of non-believers (Romans 13:13-14)
- that, because our nature is naturally sinful, we cannot *live the way God wants us to* unless we submit our hearts to God to be changed (Romans 7:14-25, 8:5-14)

Day 51

Heart-to-Heart

Bible Subject: Knowing God, God's Word

Today's Reading: Luke 10:38-41

Today's Verse: "Only one thing is needed. Mary has chosen what is better, and it will not be taken away from her." Luke 10:42

Today's Lesson: *Mary chose to know Jesus in a deeply personal way.*

We gotta have a heart-to-heart! As women, we crave relationship. And what grows a relationship better than a deep personal talk with a dear friend—a conversation so intimate that we both feel we've shared the very center of ourselves: our hearts? If we know someone's heart, we feel we *really* know them! "A [person's] heart reflects the [person]," says Proverbs 27:9.

When Mary sat at Jesus' feet listening to Him, Jesus said she had chosen what was better. What did Mary choose? To *really* know Jesus. To listen to Him so closely and attentively that she could get at the center of who He was—His heart.

Jesus wants us to know Him so well that we know His heart. In Matthew 11:29, He invites us to "come and learn of Me, for I am gentle and humble in heart." How do we learn of Jesus? The same way Mary did. By listening to what He says. And through Jesus, we can also know God. He wants us to! "I have revealed your very Self—your real Self—to the people you have given me," Jesus prays in John 17:6. (Amplified).

Amazing! God wants us to know Him in a deeply, personal way—to get at His heart! The way we do it is by listening to what He says in His Word—the Bible. "Out of the overflow of a [person's] heart, his mouth speaks," Jesus says in Luke 6:45.

The Bible tells us what's in God's heart: love and faithfulness (Psalm 119:90, Proverbs 3:3-4), compassion (Lamentations 3:22), goodness (Lamentations 3:25), mercy (Jer. 33:11), gentleness and humility (John 11:29), peace (John 14:27), kindness (Isaiah 43:13), righteousness and justice (Isaiah 42:6,3), knowledge and understanding (Jeremiah. 3:15). Whenever we read and study God's Word, we're getting to know Him better and better—we're getting at His heart.

Let's have a heart-to-heart with God today!

Prayer: Dear God, You have an amazing heart. Thank You for Your heart and love for me. I want to know You more and I want to receive all You have for me. I give You my heart today.

Day 51

For more understanding:

To learn more about understanding God's heart, you can read:

- that God wants to hold us close to *His heart* (Isaiah 40:11)
- that God wants our spiritual leaders to be examples to us of what's in *His heart* (Jeremiah 3:15)
- that the more we dedicate our hearts to God, the more we understand what's in *His heart* (Matt. 5:8)

To learn more about how God wants to know us, you can read

- that God *knows us* before we're even born (Psalm 139:13-16)
- that God *knows us* so well He *knows* how many hairs we have on our heads (Luke 12:7)
- that God so deeply wants to *know us* that He sent Jesus so that we could have a personal relationship with Him (John 14:23)

To learn more about knowing God, you can read

- that when we listen to Jesus it shows that we *know Him* (John 10:14)
- that by knowing Jesus, we *know God* (John 17:6, 29)
- that *knowing God* is the very definition of eternal life (John 17:3)

Day 52

Soul Food

Bible Subject: God's Word, Spiritual Nourishment

Today's Reading: Luke 10:38-42

Today's Verses: "Mary has chosen the good portion, that which is to her advantage, which shall not be taken away from her." Luke 10:42 (Amplified)

"You are my portion, O Lord; I have promised to keep your Word." Psalm 119:57

Today's Lesson: *Mary realized the advantage of knowing God's Word.*

Eat your candy! Did you ever hear *that* at the dinner table when you were a kid? Not likely! What you probably heard was this: Eat your vegetables! Why? Because they're good for you! Of course, eating what's good for you doesn't appeal much to kids. They don't under-stand the advantage. They'd much rather eat what tastes good than what's good for their bodies.

We can be the same way with God's Word. Sometimes we act like children spiritually and resist studying God's Word, because we don't understand the advantage. Mary knew the advantage. She knew that listening to Jesus was the most important thing she could do, so she made it a priority in her life.

We can live without vegetables, but we won't be healthy. We need proper nourishment to sustain our bodies and help us grow. We need spiritual nourishment, too, and we get it from God's Word. Knowing God's Word is vital to our spiritual health. That's why the Bible often compares God's Word to food. "[A person] does not live by bread alone, but by every word that comes from the mouth of God," Jesus tells the crowd in Matthew 4:4. In Hebrews 5:11-12, Paul tells a church that they need a solid foundation in God's Word in order to grow up spiritually. Stop drinking only milk, and start eating meat, he advises them. He's telling them that they should be mature enough spiritually to teach others about God's Word, but they still need teaching themselves.

We can't grow spiritually if we don't consume the "meat" God gives us in His Word. Just as vegetables give our bodies an advantage, when we take in God's Word and make it a part of our lives, we get an advantage, too—a blessing from God that we can never lose (Jeremiah 15:14).

Prayer: Oh, Lord Jesus. Your Word is precious and so necessary for my soul! Feed me today with Your wonderful words of truth. Help me desire Your Word more than anything else!

Day 52

For more understanding:

To learn more about how the Bible compares God's Word to food, you can read:

- that we can taste the goodness of the *Word of God* (Heb. 6:4-5)
- that we need *God's Word* as much as we need bread (Matthew 4:4)
- that we should all desire the spiritual milk of *God's Word* (1 Peter 2:2)

To learn more about the blessing we get from God's Word , you can read

- that we receive the gift of God's grace when we make *His Word* a part of our lives (Psalm 119:56)
- that Jesus Himself is the *Word of God* (John 1:14,16)
- that having the *Word of Christ* in our hearts enriches us (Col. 3:16)

To learn more about the advantage of knowing God's Word, you can read

- that knowing *God's Word* keeps us from sinning (Psalm 119:11)
- that *God's Word* gives us guidance (Psalm 119:105)
- that knowing *God's Word* helps us be effective Christians and produce fruit for God's kingdom (Mark 4:20)

Day 53

Spiritual Street Smarts

Bible Subject: Spiritual Understanding, Wisdom, Waiting on God, Worship

Today's Reading: Luke 10:38-41, John 11:1-45

Today's Verses: "[Mary] sat at the Lord's feet, listening to what He said . . ." Luke 10:39

"Mary sat still in the house [waiting for Jesus]." John 11:20b (KJV)

"When Mary reached the place where Jesus was, she fell at His feet . . ." John 11:32

Today's Lesson: *Mary always focused her attention on Jesus.*

When my kids were growing up, *Annie* was a favorite movie in our house. How could you not admire plucky Little Orphan Annie? She never went to school a day in her life, but she had street smarts that could get her out of any jam.

If Mary had lived today, we might say that she had *spiritual* street smarts. She seemed to have a spiritual savvy that other people didn't have. The Bible calls this spiritual wisdom or understanding. No matter what Mary did, she always seemed to please Jesus. And He often held Mary up as an example for other people to follow [see Luke 10:42, John 12:7, Matthew 26:13, Mark 14:9]

What did Mary know that we should know? She always focused her attention on Jesus! She knew how to make the most of the time she had with Him. Mary spent time listening to Jesus (Luke 10:39), waiting on Jesus (John 11:20b0, and worshipping Jesus (John 11:32, 12:3). The Bible tells us that each of these components is essential to spiritual understanding. God also promises that for doing each one, we will be richly rewarded.

Say *what*? We get spiritual smarts *and* a reward, too? How?

Here's what we have to do: first, *listen to God*. Knowing God's Word makes us "wise for salvation," says 2 Timothy 3:15-16. Second, *wait on God*. When the Bible speaks of "waiting on God," it almost always means an expectant waiting that is synonymous with faith. Isaiah promises that those who wait on God "will renew their strength and [become] close to God" (40:13, Amplified). Third, *worship God*. When we "exalt the Lord," says Isaiah 33:5-6, we receive "a rich store of salvation, wisdom, and knowledge." Then the Lord becomes "our strength" (v.2).

Wow! Strength, salvation, wisdom, knowledge, good works—all ours when we're spiritually smart! I want in on that deal, don't you?

Prayer: Lord Jesus, I ask for spiritual understanding. Show me how to listen, how to wait, and how to worship you in the way that You desire.

Day 53

For more understanding:

To learn more about how listening to God makes us spiritually wise, you can read:

- that God is the only one is *truly wise* (1 Tim. 1:17, Jude 25)
- that God's Word is trustworthy and makes us *wise* (Psalm 19:7)
- that God's Word itself is *wisdom* (1 Cor. 1:18-29)

To learn more about what waiting on God means, you can read

- that *we're waiting on God* when we put our hope in Him to take action in response to our prayers (Jeremiah 14:22)
- that we're *waiting on God* when we look expectantly to Him to deliver us from trouble (Gen. 49:18)
- that we're *waiting on God* when we seek guidance from His Word (Isaiah 26:7-8)

To learn more about what it means to worship God, you can read

- that we're *worshipping God* when we attribute to Him the glory that rightfully belongs to Him because of Who He is (Psalm 29:2)
- that we're *worshipping God* when we go to Him to enjoy His beauty (Psalm 27:4)
- that we're *worshipping God* when we acknowledge and stand in awe of His holiness (Isaiah 29:23)

Day 54

Present!

Bible Subject: God's Presence, Waiting for God in Terrible Times

Today's Reading: John 11:1-45

Today's Verses: "Martha whispered to Mary, 'The Teacher is present and calls you.'" John 11:28 (Young's Literal Translation)

"This is the Lord. We have waited for Him; we will be glad and rejoice in [Him]." Isaiah 25:9

Today's Lesson: *In a terrible time in her life, Mary recognized that Jesus' presence was what she needed.*

Most of us cannot imagine a more terrible tragedy than the untimely death of someone we love. Mary and her sister Martha had experienced the worst that could happen: in the prime of his life, their beloved brother Lazarus had died. Now the sisters were waiting for Jesus. How hard it must have been for Mary to wait, when her anguish, no doubt, "outweigh[ed] the sands of the sea" (Job 6:2-3).

Surely Mary knew what Jesus had said about grieving: "Blessed are they that mourn, for they shall be comforted"(Matthew 5:4). But it must have been as difficult for Mary as it is for us to see how a blessing can come out of tragedy.

In times of tragedy, our grief consumes us. God may seem far away, and a blessing even farther. Yet we can *receive a blessing when we mourn. When we're laid low by tragedy, we can see our need for God, like no other time in our life. That's the blessing—we recognize our need, and we wait on God so He can fill it with His presence. There's healing in the quietness and stillness of spiritual waiting, because then we experience God for who He really is. "Be still and know that I am God," says Psalm 49:10. When we experience God, we're in His presence, and in God's presence is "fullness of joy" (Psalm 16:11).*

In the midst of her grief, Mary "sat still in the house," (v.20, KJV) waiting for Jesus to come, and when He drew near, she responded to His presence. She jumped up and went to meet Him, opening her empty heart to Him to be comforted. This is why Jesus came: to "comfort all who mourn . . . and provide consolation and joy to those who grieve" (Isaiah 61:1,3 Amplified).

In our own terrible times, we, like Mary, can find comfort and joy in God's presence.

Prayer: Oh my God, how I need You in my times of trouble! Draw near to me with your presence!

Day 54

For more understanding:

To learn more about how God can turn mourning into joy, you can read:

- that the spiritual beauty God gives us can turn our *mourning* into gladness (Jeremiah. 31:12-14)
- that when we turn to God in our *mourning,* He promises to give us spiritual blessing (Jeremiah 31:9)
- that in God's presence, we obtain joy and gladness and all *sorrow* flees away (Isaiah 35:10)

To learn more about how spiritual waiting heals our souls, you can read:

- that when we *wait on the Lord,* we experience His mercy and lovingkindness (Lamentations 3:22-25)
- that when we *wait on God,* we experience His goodness and our heart becomes stout and enduring (Psalm 27:13-14, Amplified)
- that when we *wait on God,* we experience the sweetness and comfort of His lovingkindness (Psalm 69:6,16)

To learn more about experiencing joy in God's presence, you can read:

- that in *God's presence* is singing and gladness (Psalm 100:2)
- that in *God's presence* we experience joy and thanksgiving (Psalm 95:3)
- that all creation rejoices in the *presence of God* (Psalm 96:11-13)

Day 55

Expecting

Bible Subject: Waiting for God in Terrible Times, Hope

Today's Reading: John 11:1-45

Today's Verses: "Mary sat still in the house [until] . . . Martha whispered in her ear, "The Teacher is here and is asking for you."" John 11:20, 29 (NIV and The Message).

"Therefore we will wait expectantly for You." Jeremiah 14:22, Amplified

Today's Lesson: *In a terrible time in her life, Mary waited on Jesus with an expectant hope.*

For a mother-to-be, those nine months of expecting your blessed event can seem the longest of your life. Yet once that precious baby appears, the agony of waiting instantly turns to joy! Our pregnancies may seem endless, but we're willing to wait them out—maybe not patiently!— because of the hope we have of the wonderful promise of new life ahead.

Waiting is hard, any time in our life. But when we've experienced tragedy, like Mary had after her brother died, waiting can feel unbearable. Especially when we feel there's no hope for our life without the person we love. Yet the Bible promises that in waiting we'll find strength—and hope. "Those who wait for the Lord, who expect, look for, and hope in Him shall renew their strength," says Isaiah 40:31 (Amplified). Psalm 62:7 tells us that God is our "Rock of unyielding strength," when we wait upon Him in expectation and hope (v. 5, KJV). Biblical waiting is the same thing as having hope— hoping in God, expecting Him come to help us. That's what Mary did. Even in the midst of her grief, she sat still in the Spirit, waiting for Jesus to come. And her wait was rewarded, when Martha whispered in her ear, "He's here!"

When *we* wait on God, expectantly hoping in Him, we too know that our wait will be rewarded. God promises that His own Spirit will come to our aid, to "bear us up in our weakness" (Romans 8:28, Amplified). Imagine! In the midst of our pain and grief, God Himself comes to help us! If we're sitting still in the spirit and expectantly waiting for Him, like Mary was, we can't help but hear Him when He speaks.

As soon as we need Jesus, He's already on His way to meet us!

Prayer: Dear Jesus, I turn to You to renew my strength when I feel hopeless. Meet me where I am, as I wait expectantly for You.

Day 55

For more understanding:

To learn more about waiting for God during terrible times, you can read:

- that God promises to remove our sorrows when we *wait for Him* (Zephaniah 3:8a,16,18; Amplified)
- that when we're in distress and we *wait for God*, He comes to meet us with His strength and steadfast love (Psalm 59:9-10)
- that gives us hope through His Word when we *wait on Him* (Psalm 130:5)

To learn more about how God gives us hope during terrible times, you can read

- that when we *hope* in God we will never be disappointed, even when it seems that everyone is against us (Psalm 25:2-3, Amp.)
- that God gives us *hope* for our future even when we're mourning (Jeremiah 31:15-16)
- that God gives us *hope* in his Word when we're suffering (Psalm 199:147, 153)

To learn more about how God helps us when we're weak, you can read

- that God is our refuge *when we're weak* (Joel 3:10b, 16b)
- that we can rely on God's strength *when we're weak* (2 Corinthians 12:9)
- that *when we're weak and fearful* God comes to save us (Isaiah 35:3-4)

Day 56

The Energizer

Bible Subject: God's Word in Terrible Times

Today's Reading: John 11:1-44

Today's Verses: "As soon as Mary heard [that Jesus was asking for her], she sprang up quickly and came unto Him." John 11:29 (KJV and Amplified)

"Revive and stimulate me according to Your Word." (Psalm 119:25, KJV and Amplified)

Today's Lesson: *During a terrible time in her life, Mary responded to God's Word.*

My son is fascinated by "roly-polies," those tiny millipede-like "bugs" who roll up into tight little balls when they feel threatened. Their crusty outer skeleton is the creature's defense mechanism—the way they protect themselves from a dangerous world.

Terrible times in our lives can make *us* act like roly-polies. We can turn inward and hide away in our shells, because interacting with the world is just too dangerous to our damaged souls. Mary was no different. After her brother Lazarus died, Mary sat alone and silent among the houseful of people who had come to comfort her. But when her sister Martha told Mary that Jesus was asking for her, Mary immediately "jumped up and ran to meet Him" (John 11:29, The Message). Even in the midst of her grief, Mary responded to God's Word.

In our worst times, truthfully, we may feel more like ignoring God's Word than responding to it. Yet, even when our spirits are so low that our soul "cleaves to the dust," God's Word has the power to "revive and stimulate" us (Psalm 119:25, KJV and Amplified). "For the Word that God speaks is alive and full of power," says Hebrews 4:12 (Amplified), "making it energizing and effective." To be *energized*—just what we need when we feel dead inside from grief. We have God's promise that His Word *always* accomplishes the purpose for which He sends it (Isaiah 55:11). And when are hearts are burdened with sorrow, the purpose God intends for His Word is that our burdens be lifted and our sorrow replaced with the joy only He can give us (Matthew 11:30, Psalm 68:19).

The Bible tells us that God's Word "revives the soul" and "gives joy to the heart" (Psalm 19:7-8).

In the terrible times of our lives, God's Word is the best medicine we could ever have!

Prayer: My God, I thank You that Your Word has the power to revive and strengthen me in terrible times. I give You all my burdens today.

Day 56

For more understanding:

To learn more about how God's Word revives us in terrible times, you can read:

- that *God's Word revives us* when we're in trouble (Psalm 138:2b,7)
- that *God's Word revives* our spirit when we're mourning (Isaiah 57:14-15,18)
- that *God's Word revives us* so that we can rejoice in hard times (Psalm 85:6,8)

To learn more about how God replaces our sorrow with joy, you can read:

- that God creates *joyful praise* on our lips even when we're mourning (Isaiah 57:19)
- that through Jesus we *obtain a joy* that chases away sorrow (Isaiah 35:10)
- that God promises gives us so many spiritual blessings, we'll be *filled with comfort and joy* instead of sorrow (Jeremiah 31:12-14)

To learn more about how God rescues us from our burdens, you can read

- that God daily *carries our burdens* for us (Psalm 68:19)
- that God sustains us when we *give up our burdens* to Him (Psalm 55:12)
- that as believers we're supposed to help *bear each others' burdens* (Galatians 6:2)

Day 57

My Pleasure

Bible Subject: Pleasing God

Today's Reading: John 12:1-11; Matthew 26:6-13, Mark 14:1-10

Today's Verses: "Why are you bothering this woman? She has done a praiseworthy and beautiful thing for Me." Matthew 26:10, Amplified

"Try to learn in your experience what is pleasing to the Lord." Ephesians 5:10

Today's Lesson: *Mary cared more about pleasing Jesus than about pleasing other people.*

Are you a people-pleaser? Most of us women are, to some extent. We're nurturers at heart, and that means we want to make other people happy. Nothing wrong with that—unless we're so eager to please other people, we forget that our first priority should be to please God.

Mary never forgot to please God first, and it got her in trouble with other people. Her sister Martha didn't like it (Luke 10:38-41), and neither did Jesus' disciples. At Simon's dinner party given in honor of Jesus, the disciples were outraged at Mary's "waste" of the expensive perfume she poured on Jesus' head (Matthew 26:8). They murmured and gossiped about her behind her back, and criticized her so harshly that Jesus had to step in and defend her. And He did far more than defend her—He told them what she had done was so noteworthy that it would be retold wherever the Gospel was preached, in memory of her. "She has done a beautiful thing for Me," Jesus said (Matthew 26:10-13). What was the "beautiful thing"? I believe it was Mary's desire to please Jesus above all else. God loves it when we honor Him by putting Him first, when pleasing Him is more important than anything else. "I have esteemed and treasured [what God wants me to do] more than my necessary food," says Job 23:12.

When we desire to please God more than pleasing other people, it's a pleasure to *Him* (Psalm 104:34). In fact, the Bible tells us that pleasing God with our attitude of heart is the most excellent thing we can do (Proverbs 31:30).

May our attitude of heart be as beautiful to Jesus as Mary's was!

Prayer: Dear Jesus, I want to please You in all I do! Help me honor You by putting You first in my life.

Day 57

For more understanding:

To learn more about how to please God, you can read:

- that we *please God* when we seek him earnestly (Isaiah 26:9)
- that we *please God* when we live in a way that honors Him (Ephesians 5:10)
- that we *please God* when our prayers are full of rejoicing (Psalm 104:34)

To learn more about how to put God first, you can read

- that *God* should be our *first* and greatest love (Rev. 2:4)
- that seeking the spiritual benefits of doing things *God's way* rather than our own should be our *first and greatest concern* (Matthew 6:33)
- that *God* is the *first and the last* of everything (Isaiah 44:6, Rev. 22:13, Amp.)

To learn more about having an attitude of heart that pleases God, you can read:

- that a humble and thankful heart *pleases God* (Psalm 69:30-32)
- that a heart full of mercy, love, and truth *pleases God* (Proverbs 16:6-7)
- that an attitude of reverence and worshipful awe towards God *pleases Him* (Psalm 147:11)

Day 58

Spiritual Princesses

Bible Subject: True Worship

Today's Reading: John 12:1-11; Matthew 26:6-13

Today's Verse: "She has done a noble thing to Me." Matthew 26:10

"Many women do noble things, but you surpass them all . . . [for a] woman who reverently and worshipfully fears the Lord, she shall be praised!" Proverbs 31:29-30 (NIV and Amplified)

Today's Lesson: *Mary gave Jesus the true worship that God desires*

Little girls often dream of growing up to be a princess. And when we do grow up, most of us certainly wouldn't mind being treated *like one! Maybe we can't be real-life princesses, but we* can *be nobility—spiritually, anyway.*

How do we get to be spiritual princesses? The Bible asks the same question—and answers it. "A noble woman who can find?" asks Proverbs 31:10 (KJV and NIV). "She is far more precious than jewels and her value is far above rubies or pearls." The Amplified Bible makes it clear that the noble woman described in Proverbs 31 is being measured not by status, wealth, ability, or physical virtue, but by her spiritual and practical devotion to God*—her true worship of the Lord. The Bible calls this reverence.

Jesus tells us in John 4:23 that God is actively seeking true worshippers—those who will worship Him in spirit and truth. All this means is that God wants only worship that's sincere and whole-hearted. And Mary knew how to worship Jesus that way!

Giving God honor and worshipping Him are the same thing. "Give unto the Lord the honor of His name," says Psalm 29:20 (KJV). "Worship the Lord in the beauty of holiness." True worship, then, means we honor God in everything we do, say, and think, and we count everything else in our lives as secondary to Him.

This is what Mary did. When Mary poured rare and costly perfume on Jesus feet, the "whole house was filled with the fragrance" (v. 3). Not a soul present would have had any doubt about the extent of Mary's honor for Jesus!

We don't have to go to church to worship God the way He wants. We can worship Him anywhere and anytime, when our thoughts, our words, and our actions honor Him.

Prayer: Oh God, teach me how to worship You every day in everything that I do.

*See footnotes for Proverbs 31:10-31 in the Amplified Bible.

Day 58

For more understanding:

To learn more about worshiping God whole-heartedly (in spirit), you can read:

- that worshipping God whole-heartedly gives us spiritual freedom (2 Cor. 3:17)
- that worshipping God with our whole spirit helps us ilve our lives in a way that pleases God (Gal. 5:25)
- that worshipping God whole-heartedly helps us know God better (Phil.3:8)

To learn more about worshipping God sincerely (in truth), you can read

- that when we worship God sincerely, God reveals Himself to us (John 1:18)
- that God doesn't want worship that's not sincere (Matt. 15:8-9)
- that to worship sincerely we must follow God's teaching rather than other people's (Matt. 15:9)

To learn more about being spiritually noble, you can read

- that we're spiritually noble when we delight in God's Word (Psalm 112:1)
- that we're spiritually noble when we love and obey God (Deut. 10:12)
- that we're spiritually noble when we trust God (1Tim. 1:5, Ampl.)

Day 59

Can Do

Bible Subject: Honoring God

Today's Reading: Mark 14:3-9; John 12:1-11; Matthew 26:6-13

Today's Verse: "She has done what she could." Mark 14:18

Today's Lesson: Mary was willing to sacrifice her own self-interest in order to honor Jesus.

Self-interest comes as naturally to us as breathing. Nowhere is that fact more evident than in a toddler's howl "Mine! Mine!" and the tantrum that follows. As humans, we're naturally inclined to seek what's best for ourselves. But at the dinner in Bethany given in Jesus' honor, Mary did the opposite.* She sacrificed her own self-interest in order to honor Jesus.

When Mary poured expensive perfume on Jesus head and wiped his feet with her hair, it would have been considered a scandalous act by everyone at the party, probably even her own sister and brother. Think about it. Mary's family was not wealthy, yet she had spent *an entire year's wages* on the perfume!** Who knows but that it was money set aside for her own wedding dowry? Not only did Mary sacrifice the money she could have kept for herself, she sacrificed her own reputation, most likely even her prospects for making a good marriage. Who would want to marry a woman who debased herself by wiping a man's feet with her hair?

Mary was willing to sacrifice what was important to her personally in order to give Jesus the honor and glory he deserved. Are we willing to do the same? We don't have to spend a year's wages to honor Jesus. God doesn't expect us to! Jesus said that Mary did "what she could" (Mark 14:18). That's all God asks of us—to do what we can, however small or large. The Bible tells us that we should set aside our self-interests in order to serve Jesus with our whole hearts: "Let us throw off every unnecessary weight, looking away from all that distracts, to Jesus, the Leader and Source of our faith . . ." (Hebrews 12:1-2, Amplified).

What can we do in our lives today that will honor Jesus?

Prayer: Dear Jesus, help me to do what I can do honor You, even if it means making sacrifices.

---

*Although Mary is not named in Mark 14 or Matthew 26 as the woman with the alabaster jar, John 12 tells the same story and *does* name the woman as Mary of Bethany.

**300 denarii was equal to a laboring man's wages for a year. See Mark 14:5 (Amplified).

Day 59

For more understanding:

To learn more about honoring God, you can read:

- that we *honor God* when we open our hearts to His Word (John 5:23)
- that we *honor God* when our hearts and minds are focused on Him (Isaiah 29:13, Amp)
- that we honor God when we trust Him completely (1 Tim. 1:17-19)

To learn more about sacrificing our own self-interest, you can read

- that God wants us to offer to Him the spiritual *sacrifice of dedicating our life* completely to Him (1 Peter 2:5, Amplified)
- that Jesus *sacrificed His own self-interest* when He willingly died for us (Ephesians 5:2, Amplified)
- that God is pleased when we *sacrifice our own self-interest* in order to be kind and generous to the needy (Hebrews 13:16)

To learn more about serving Jesus wholeheartedly, you can read

- that we *serve Jesus* when we do everything as if we were doing it for Him (Col. 3:23-24)
- that we *serve Jesus* by conforming wholly to His example in living (John 12:26, Amp.)
- that we *serve Jesus* when we rely on him rather than on our money (Luke 16:13)

Day 60

Urgent!

Bible Subject: Salvation, Spiritual Urgency

Today's Reading: John 12:1-11; Matthew 26:6-13; Mark 14:3-9

Today's Verses: "Wherever this Gospel is preached throughout the world, what she has done will be told in memory of her." Matthew 26:13

"You know what a critical hour this is, how it is high time for you to awake out of sleep, to rouse to reality, for now is our salvation near . . ." Romans 13:11 (Amplified Bible)

Today's Lesson: Mary understood the urgency of having a relationship with Jesus.

When we see a letter, an email, or a text marked *urgent,* we know it's a message that can't wait. It's *important.* We have to do something about it *now,* or there may be consequences in our lives that we won't want to face. The same is true in our spiritual lives. Some things in our spiritual lives are urgent, and can't be put off—like having a relationship with Jesus.

At the supper in Bethany given for Jesus, Mary seemed to be the only person in the house who understood the urgency of making her relationship with Jesus the most important thing in her life. When she poured expensive perfume over His head, Mary was showing that she was willing to do whatever it took to honor Jesus, even if it meant being ridiculed and scorned by other people—like the disciples and Judas Iscariot. Mary knew that there was no time to waste in surrendering her entire life to Jesus. Her relationship with Jesus was far more valuable to her than the cost of the perfume—an entire year's paycheck*. Mary put her relationship with Jesus first, above everything else in her life, and she did it *now*.

That's what Jesus wants us to do, too. In Revelation 3:20, Jesus told a church full of people that He was standing at the door of their heart, constantly knocking. "If anyone hears Me calling him and opens the door," Jesus says, "I will come in and fellowship with him and he with Me" (Living Bible).

Jesus is inviting us *now* to have a relationship with Him. And *now* is the time that we must make a decision whether or not we will accept His invitation."Right now God is ready to welcome you," says 2 Corinthians 6:2. "Today He is ready to save you" (Living Bible). God wants to give us salvation *today*, so that we can enter into a relationship with Him.

What will our answer be?

Prayer: Dear Jesus, I accept your invitation to have a relationship with You. I want to receive Your salvation, and I open my heart to You to come into my life. Help me make You the most important thing in my life.

---

*300 denarii—the cost of the perfume Mary poured on Jesus' head—was equal to a laboring man's wages for a year. See Mark 14:5 (Amplified).

Day 60

For more understanding:

To learn more about salvation, you can read

- that *salvation* is a gift from God that we can't earn (Ephesians 2:8)
- that God makes *salvation* available to everyone and He wants everyone to receive it (John 3:16-17, 1 Timothy 2:4)
- that all we have to do to receive *salvation* is believe in Jesus and surrender control of our lives to Him (John 3:16-17)

To learn more about what happens when we accept Jesus' invitation to receive salvation, you can read:

- that *receiving salvation* means God forgives of our sins and releases us from all judgment and condemnation that results from our sin (John 3:18)
- that *receiving salvation* means God gives us eternal life (John 3:16)
- that *receiving salvation* means God adopts us as His children so that we can have a relationship with Him (Hebrews 2:10)

To learn more about how much God wants us to have a relationship with Him, you can read

- that God's love for us is so great, He gives us salvation so that we can *fellowship with Him* (Ephesians 2:4-5)
- that God rejoices when we accept Him as our Saviour and delights in having a *relationship* with us (Zephaniah 3:17)
- that God takes pleasure in having a *relationship* with His people (Psalm 149:4)

For Deeper Thought

Questions for Discussion and Reflection

Elizabeth's Story

Read about Elizabeth in the Bible in Luke 1:5-66 and Lessons 1-8 in *Blessed Is She.*

1. Who was Elizabeth and what was she like? Was she someone you would have enjoyed knowing? Why or why not?

2. What's the first thing the Bible tells us about Elizabeth? Why do you think that is important for us to know?

3. Who do you think had a stronger faith in God—Elizabeth or her husband Zachariah? Why?

4. What clues does the Bible give us about Elizabeth's relationship with God? What do you think "powered" Elizabeth's relationship with God? What benefits did Elizabeth gain from her relationship with God?

5. What was Elizabeth great hardship in life and how had it affected her? Do you think her hardship had changed Elizabeth for the better, for the worse, or not at all?

6. Have you or someone you've known suffered a hardship that was life-changing? Explain.

7. In Luke 1:25, Elizabeth says that her pregnancy had taken away her "reproach" among people. What does Elizabeth mean by this? Why do you think Elizabeth's infertility had made her feel under reproach? What hardships that people suffer today can still bring reproach on them? Why do you think this is?

8. Sometimes today we still take a "blame the victim" mentality toward people's hardships. Why do you think we do that? What do you think our response toward people suffering hardship *should* be?

Mary's Story

Read about Mary in the Bible in Matthew 1:18-2:12, Luke 1:26-2:52, John 2:1-11, John 19:23-30, Acts 1:14, and Lessons 9-35 in *Blessed Is She.*

1. Why do you think God chose Mary—a teenage girl living in a dusty, obscure little village—to be the mother of His Son, Jesus? What made Mary different from other young women?

2. What does Mary's song (Luke 1:46-55) tell us about what kind of person Mary was? What does it tell us about her relationship with God?

3. What clues does Mary's story give us about how to have a right relationship with God? What most impresses you about how Mary's faith in God affected the way she lived her life?

4. In Luke 1:34, though Mary obviously believed what the angel was telling her, she wanted to know *how* all this would happen. Do you think it was all right for Mary to ask such a thing? Why or why not? Do you think it's all right for *us* to ask such questions of God? Why or why not?

5. Why do you think Mary was in such a hurry to go to her cousin Elizabeth's house after the angel had appeared to her? Has there been a time when God impressed upon you something that you had to do right away? What was it, and why do you think it had to be done immediately?

6. Mary's story is filled with many instances of God accomplishing the impossible in her life. What were some of them? What do we learn from Mary about God's requirement for accomplishing the impossible in *our* lives? Have you ever had something you thought was impossible happen to you? How did it affect your life?

7. What do you think it was like for Mary when she had to tell Joseph she was pregnant? Do you think Joseph believed her story at first? Put yourself in Joseph's place. Would you have believed Mary? Why or why not? Having faith in impossible things is never easy. What does it take in our lives for us to have faith?

8. Mary found out how much she needed God's wisdom as the mother of Jesus. When was a time that you discovered how much you needed God's wisdom in a situation? How do we seek God's wisdom for ourselves?

9. At the wedding in Cana, Mary turned to Jesus when she found herself in a hopeless situation. What can we learn from Mary's story about how Jesus meets our spiritual needs, as well as our physical needs, when we turn to Him for help?

10. What things do you think Mary was treasuring in her heart in Luke 2:19? How can God's Word be a treasure to us? Think about what the Bible says as well as your own experiences.

Naomi's Story

Read about Naomi in the Bible in the Book of Ruth, and Lessons 36-41 in *Blessed Is She.*

1. How do you think Naomi managed to model her faith to Ruth despite all the tragedy in Naomi's life? How can hard times affect our faith? Our witness to others *about* our faith? Have you ever been able to share your faith during a tough time in your life?

2. Naomi lived in a culture where her faith made different from everybody else. Sometimes our faith can make us different from everyone else, too. What do we do when being true to our faith means we run the risk of being unpopular, all alone, or even persecuted? Put yourself in Naomi's situation. Would you be able to openly display your faith if you were the only one doing it?

3. Do you think it's possible to experience joy in your life when you're going through difficult times? How?

4. Have you ever experienced a time of great grief like Naomi did?

ELIZABETH McDAVID JONES

How did your grief affect your faith? How did your faith affect your grief?

5. What does it mean to you that "nothing can separate us from the love of Christ," not even our circumstances? (Romans 8:35-39)

6. Waiting for something we desperately want in our lives can be one of the hardest things we ever have to do. When was a time in your life when you had to wait for something, and what was the result?

7. Have you ever felt like Naomi did, that God's hand had gone out against you? What made you feel that way? What are some instances in Naomi's story that show that Naomi still hoped in God despite her hardships?

8. Naomi received a promise at the beginning of her story and at the end of her story. What were they, and who spoke the promises to her? Do you think God can speak to us through other people? Have you experienced a time that happened to you? What are some other ways God speaks to us?

9. Imagine Naomi, a young widow, trying to raise her sons in a culture where nobody worshipped or honored God. What advice would you give Naomi and how would it help her?

Martha's Story

Read about Martha in the Bible in Luke 10:38-42 and John 13:1-17, and Lessons 42-50 in *Blessed Is She*.

1. In Luke 10:38-42, the first thing we learn about Martha is that she "opened her home" to Jesus. What does it mean to open your home to someone? What does this tell us about Martha? From what the Bible tells us about Martha, what kind of person do you think she was? Can you "paint" a character sketch of her?

2. John 11:5 says that Jesus "loved Mary and Martha and Lazarus" as dear friends. What about Martha do you think would have made her a good friend? Would you like to have had a friend more like Martha, or like her sister Mary? Why?

3. Compare Martha's way of serving God to Mary's way. Do you think one way of serving God is better than another? Why or why not?

4. Do you see yourself more as a "Martha" or a "Mary?" Explain your answer.

5. What are some other ways we can serve God? Provide your own thoughts as well as Bible verses, if you can. See Romans 12:6-11, if you need help.

6. In John 11:3-6, we read that Martha and Mary sent word to Jesus that their brother Lazarus was sick, but Jesus delayed coming until after Lazarus had died. Do you think Martha had a hard time understanding why Jesus didn't immediately respond to her request? What makes you think so? Have you had an experience like Martha's? What was it? What faith lessons did you learn from your experience?

7. In John 11:25-26, Jesus asks Martha to focus on Him rather than on her circumstances. Why is it essential for us to focus on Jesus in the terrible times of our lives? How do we do that? How does it help us to do so?

8. Psalm 33:4 tells us that God is faithful in all He does. What are some lessons Martha learned about God's faithfulness when her brother Lazarus died? Have you had an experience when God showed His faithfulness to you in a terrible time in your life? Consider sharing your experience with the group.

9. Waiting on God is one of the most difficult things we have to do in our spiritual lives. What can we learn about waiting on God from Martha's story? When was a time you had to wait on God for something you desperately wanted? How did that challenge your faith?

Mary of Bethany's Story

Read about Mary of Bethany in the Bible in Luke 10:38-42; John 11:1-45, 13:1-17; Matthew 26:6-13; Mark 14:1-10, and Lessons 50-60 in *Blessed Is She*

1. In Luke's story about Mary of Bethany, the first thing we learn about her is that she sat at Jesus' feet, listening to what He said. How does this characterize Mary? How does it show what was most important for Mary? How does Mary's example challenge you in setting priorities for your life?

2. Both Mary and her sister Martha were seeking the Lord in their own ways. What was Martha's way? What was Mary's? Which does Jesus commend most highly? Why do you think He does this? Which sister are you most like in your spiritual life, and why?

3. In Luke 1:38-42, Martha was upset with Mary because Mary wasn't doing her portion of the work providing hospitality to their guests. But Jesus tells Martha that Mary had chosen the *better* portion, that which "wouldn't be taken away from her." What do you think Jesus meant by this? How can you apply Jesus' words to your own life?

For Deeper Knowledge

An 8-Week Elizabeth Bible Study

Elizabeth Lesson One

First Things First: Continuing in Hope

Memory Verse: "Continue to stay with your faith in Jesus Christ, not moving away from the hope that rests on the Gospel." Colossians 1:23 (Amplified Bible)

Prepare: At home, read Luke Chapter 1. Memorize the week's Bible verse above.

Reflect: Read Day One, "First Things First," in *Blessed Is She*

Getting Started: Read aloud Luke 1:5-25, 57-80. Repeat the Memory Verse to yourself or together.

Study and Discuss:

1. What are some important "firsts" in your life? Why were they meaningful?

2. What is meaningful about each of the "firsts" in these verses? **Deuteronomy 21:17; John 20:1; Mark 12:28-30; Revelation 1:11; Luke 13:30; Romans 8:29**

3. Why do you think "firsts" are important to God?

4. How does our first impression of people we meet shape what we think about them? As we meet people in Scripture, we form first impressions about them as well. What are your first impressions about each woman of the Bible below? Hannah, in **1 Samuel 1:2**; Ruth, in **Ruth 1:14-17**; Deborah, in **Judges 4:4-5**; Mary, in **Luke 1:38**; Elizabeth, in **Luke 1:6**

5. First impressions are important, but we don't really understand who a person really is until we've spent time getting to know them. The same is true of people in the Bible. What do learn about Elizabeth's personality and character from the following verses? **Luke 1:19-20, 25, 43-45, 60**

6. What was Elizabeth's greatest desire in life? Had God given it to her?

7. How do you think that made Elizabeth feel about herself? About her faith? About God?

8. Do you think Elizabeth ever felt discouraged because God had not answered her prayer? Why or why not?

9. Whose faith do you think was stronger—Elizabeth's or Zachariah's? Why?

10. When we're faced with long periods of unanswered prayer, as Elizabeth was, it's easy to get discouraged and give up hope. We may begin to blame ourselves, even God. When those times come, as they invariably will, what does the Bible tell us we should do? See **John 15:10; John 8:31; Colossians 1:22-23, 4:2; II Timothy 3:14.**

Bible Truth for this lesson:

Continuing in the Lord means standing firm in the hope that Jesus gives us, even when the rest of our life may seem hopeless.

Elizabeth Lesson Two

God's Fringe Benefits: The Goodness of God

Memory Verse: "Oh God, let us rejoice in Your goodness." II Chronicles 6:41

Prepare: At home, read Luke Chapter 1. Memorize the week's Bible verse above.

Reflect: Read Day Two, "God's Fringe Benefits," in *Blessed Is She.*

Getting Started: Read aloud Luke 1:5-25, 57-80. Repeat the Memory Verse to yourself or together.

Study and Discuss:

1. Last week we talked about first impressions and how our impressions of people's character change as we get to know them better. What were some of your first impressions about God? Have those impressions changed over time? How? What are some things you've learned about God's character as you've gotten to know *Him* better?

2. God's goodness—sometimes called loving kindness in the Bible—is

one of His most important character traits. What do the following verses tell us about God's goodness? **Psalm 63:3-5, Psalm 69:16, Psalm 107:8-9**

3. Because of God's goodness, we receive many benefits when we have a relationship with Him. What are some of them? See **Psalm 103:2-5, Psalm 6:19, Psalm 145:16, Jeremiah 31:14, 1 Timothy 6:17**

4. What clues do we have in Elizabeth's story that she still believed in the goodness of God, even after so many years of hoping for something that had never come to pass?

5. Do you think it ever got hard for Elizabeth to keep trusting in God's goodness through all her years of infertility? Why or why not? Are there clues in Scripture that support your belief?

6. Was there ever a time in your life when something happened that made you question the goodness of God? Be honest with your answer.

7. Trusting in God's goodness is an important component of faith. How do the following verses reassure us that:

God is good? **Psalm 86:5, Psalm 34:8**
God desires good for us? **Psalm 103:2-5**
God *still* desires good for us, even when it doesn't seem that way?
Romans 8:28
God's goodness can satisfy us? **Psalm 107:8-9; Psalm 145:8,16**

8. Can you share a time in your life when God encouraged you with His goodness, even when you felt hopeless?

Bible Truth for this lesson:

God is good, and desires good for us, even when it doesn't seem that way.

Elizabeth Lesson Three

Too Good To Believe: Trusting in God's Word

Memory Verse: "No matter how many promises God has made, they are Yes in Christ." II Corinthians 1:20

Prepare: At home, read Luke Chapter 1. Memorize the week's Bible verse above.

Reflect: Read Day Three, "Too Good To Believe," in *Blessed Is She.*

Getting Started: Read aloud Luke 1:5-25, 57-80. Repeat the Memory Verse to yourself or together.

Study and Discuss:

1. What does trust mean to you? What does it take for you to trust someone? Has anyone that you trusted ever broken a promise to you? How do we demonstrate that we trust someone? How do we know that someone is trustworthy?

2. How do we know that God is trustworthy? See **Isaiah 45:19; Lamentations 3:21-23; Psalm 146:5-7; Hebrews 6:18**

3. Do you think Elizabeth trusted God? Why or why not? What clues did you get from the Bible for your answer?

4. Do you think Zachariah trusted God? Why do you think Zachariah had trouble believing the promise the angel made to him?

5. When someone makes a promise to you, how do you decide whether or not to believe them? If you know someone always tells the truth, how does that play into your decision? How important is it for you to know that someone always tells the truth?

6. The Bible tells us that God Himself is the very definition of Truth. How do each of the following verses reinforce that concept? **Psalm 31:5, Psalm 119:142, John 14:6, John 15:26, 1 John 5:6**

7. How do we know that we can always trust what God tells us in His Word? See **Psalm 119:138, John 17:17; Ephesians 1:13, Hebrews 6:18**

8. How do we know that God always keeps His promises to us? See **1 Kings 8:56, Psalm 105:42, 2 Corinthians 1:20, 2 Peter 1:4**

9. What does the idea of reliability mean to you? How do we measure reliability in our lives, in terms of a *reliable* vehicle, a *reliable* friend, a *reliable* significant other? What do you think is the connection between reliability and trust?

10. What do the following verses tell us about the reliability of God's Word? **2 Samuel 22:51 Psalm 18:30 Psalm 117:2 John 1:14**

Bible Truth for this lesson:

Because God is the very definition of Truth, we can trust Him and fully believe His Word to us—the Bible.

Elizabeth Lesson Four

Foxhole Christians: Giving Credit to God

Memory Verse: "The Lord has done this for me." Luke 1:25

Prepare: At home, read Luke Chapter 1. Memorize the week's Bible verse above.

Reflect: Read Day Four, "Foxhole Christians," in *Blessed Is She.*

Getting Started: Read aloud Luke 1:5-25, 57-80. Repeat the Memory Verse to yourself or together.

Study and Discuss:

1. When was a time that someone did something really wonderful for you? Did you keep it to yourself or did you tell everyone about it? Why?

2. What wonderful thing had God done for Elizabeth? Why was it important for her to give credit to God?

3. How do we nurture our human relationships? What clues does the Bible give us about how Elizabeth nurtured her relationship with

God? See **Luke 1:6, 24-25, 41, 45**

4. What happens to our human relationships when we don't appreciate each other? How do our human relationships suffer when we take each other for granted? When was a time that you took someone in your life for granted and how did it affect your relationship? Were you able to "fix" the relationship and how did you do it?

5. Our relationship with God is the most important one we'll ever have. In **Jeremiah 2:32,** the Living Bible states that God is "the most precious of our treasures." What does that statement mean to you?

6. What are some ways that we take God for granted? What happens to our relationship with Him when we do that?

7. The best way that we can avoid taking God for granted is to spend time with Him regularly. The Bible calls this "coming into God's presence." What do the following verses tell us about the benefits of spending time in God's presence? **1 Chronicles 16:27, Psalm 16:11, Psalm 51:11-12**

8. Why is it important for us to give credit to God, or acknowledge Him, for what He has done for us? See **Psalm 145:21, Matthew 10:32, 1 John 4:3**

9. **Psalm 145** is all about appreciating what God has done for us. Read the psalm aloud. What are some things the writer (David) appreciated God doing for him? List some things for which *you* appreciate God.

Bible Truth for this lesson:

Our relationship with God is too precious to be taken for granted.

Elizabeth Lesson Five

In the Name of God: Trusting in Who God Is

Memory Verse: "Some trust in chariots and horses, but we trust in the name of the Lord our God." Psalm 20:7

Prepare: At home, read Luke Chapter 1. Memorize the week's Bible verse above.

Reflect: Read Day Five, "In the Name of God," in *Blessed Is She*.

Getting Started: Read aloud Luke 1:23-25, 45, 57-63; Matthew 12:21. Repeat the Memory Verse to yourself or together.

Study and Discuss:

1. How does a person's name represent them? How important is a person's reputation? Why? Have you ever made a judgment about someone based on their reputation alone? Did you find that you were right or wrong?

2. In what ways does a person's name, or reputation, represent their

character? In what ways does God's name, or reputation, represent His character? See **Luke 1:49, Psalm 8:1, Isaiah 9:6 (KJV)**

3. How did Elizabeth show that she trusted in God's reputation, or character?

4. How do each of these verses show that we can trust in God's character, in Who He is? **Psalm 3:12, 10:17, 17:7; Matthew 12:21**

5. How is God's character represented by His Name? See **Psalm 8:1; Isaiah 9:6 (KJV); Luke 1:49**

6. Why is it important for us to trust in God's reputation by trusting in His Name? See **Psalm 23:3, 106:8; 1 John 2:12**

7. How is *believing in* someone the same as trusting in their character, or who they are? What makes us "believe" in someone? Who are some people that you would say you believe in, and why do you feel that way about them?

8. How do we know that we can *believe in* God's Name?

9. What happens to us when we believe in God's Name? See **Joel 2:32; John 1:12; Romans 10:13; 1 John 3:23**

10. How does Elizabeth's story reassure us that *we* can trust in God's Name, like she did?

Bible Truth for this lesson:

Because we know God's Character, we know we can trust Him.

Elizabeth Lesson Six

Confidence in Confidence: Putting Our Confidence in God

Memory Verse: "Be confident in the Lord with all your heart . . ." Proverbs 3:26, Amplified Bible

Prepare: At home, read Luke Chapter 1. Memorize the week's Bible verse above.

Reflect: Read Day Six, "Confidence in Confidence," in *Blessed Is She*.

Getting Started: Read aloud Luke 1:39-45, 59-63. Repeat the Memory Verse to yourself or together.

Study and Discuss:

1. Sharing a confidence means we trust someone. When was a time you shared a confidence with someone that you would never tell anyone else? How did you choose that person to put your confidence in? How did you know that you could trust him or her?

2. Have you ever put your confidence in someone and that person let you down? How did that make you feel?

3. The Bible tells us that when we put our confidence in God, He never lets us down. What does each of the following verses say to you about having confidence in God? **Psalm 65:5; Ephesians 1:12, 3:12; Hebrews 4:16**

4. How did Elizabeth show her confidence in the Lord?

5. How do each of the following verses tell us why we should put our confidence in God? **Hebrews 3:6,14; 1 John 3:21-22, 5:14**

6. We could call Psalm 118 the Confidence in God Psalm. Read the entire psalm aloud. Then explain how each of the following verses tells why we should we put our confidence in God instead of in people: **v.1,6,8-9,14, 21**

7. Who makes it possible for us to be confident in our relationship with God? **Ephesians 3:11-12, Hebrews 4:14-16**

8. What does having confidence in God look like in our daily lives?

9. What are some things that we put our confidence in instead of God? What is the result when we do that? How can you begin today to put your confidence in God instead?

Bible Truth for this lesson:

When we trust God, we put our confidence in Him instead of in ourselves or in other things.

Elizabeth Lesson Seven

The Gift that Keeps on Giving: The Holy Spirit

Memory Verse: "If you [people] know how to give good gifts to your children, how much more will your heavenly Father give the Holy Spirit to those who ask Him." Luke 11:13

Prepare: At home, read Luke Chapter 1. Memorize the week's Bible verse above.

Reflect: Read Day Seven, "The Gift that Keeps on Giving," in *Blessed Is She.*

Getting Started: Read aloud Luke 1:26-56. Repeat the Memory Verse to yourself or together.

Study and Discuss:

1. What is the most special gift you've ever received? What made the gift so special?

2. Have you ever re-gifted anyone with a gift you'd gotten from someone else? Why did you decide to re-gift the person? How was the

re-gift received by that person? How would you feel about getting a re-gift yourself if you knew it was a re-gift? Explain your answer.

3. The Holy Spirit is a gift that God gives to us that we're *supposed* to re-gift to others. What is special about God's gift of His own Spirit to us? See **John 14:16-17, Acts 2:17-18, 1 Corinthians 2:9-10, 12:11, Colossians 1:8**

4. Why does God want to give us His own Spirit in the first place? See **John 14:16, Hebrews 2:4, Colossians 1:9-12**

5. What does the Holy Spirit do for us? **John 14:16, 1 Corinthians 2:10-12**

6. What are some of the gifts that the Holy Spirit gives to us? **Acts 2:17-18, 1 Corinthians 12:1-13; Galatians 5:22-23**

7. Read the following verses aloud. What do these verses tell us about some of the ways we're supposed to re-gift the gifts of the Spirit to others? **Romans 12:6-8, 1 Corinthians 12:28-31, 14:1-33, 1 Peter 4:10-11**

8. How did both Elizabeth and Mary re-gift the Holy Spirit to other people?

9. According to **1 Corinthians 13:1-14:1** which gift of the Holy Spirit is the most to be desired? Why is this gift the greatest of all the spiritual gifts?

Bible Truth for this lesson:

God gives us the gift of His Spirit so that we can re-gift them to other people.

Elizabeth Lesson Eight

God's Secret Ingredient: Knowing God's Word

Memory Verse: "Your words are what sustain me: they are food to my hungry soul." Jeremiah 15:16, Living Bible

Prepare: At home, read Luke Chapter 1. Memorize the week's Bible verse above.

Reflect: Read Day Eight, "God's Secret Ingredient," in *Blessed Is She.*

Getting Started: Read aloud Luke 1:5-7, 24-25, 41-45, 57-63. Repeat the Memory Verse to yourself or together.

Study and Discuss:

1. What are some of your favorite foods to cook and to eat? Why are they your favorite? What is a favorite *comfort* food—something you like to eat or make when there's a certain need in your life? Why does that particular food give you comfort or make you feel better?

2. **Psalm 119:50** says that God's Word is a comfort to us when we're in

trouble. How can God's Word be like a comfort food to us? Use the Bible as well as your own experiences to answer.

3. How might Elizabeth have found comfort from God's Word during her long years of infertility? How did Elizabeth show that God's Word was an important part of her life?

4. The Bible often compares God's Word to food. Look up the following verses to see how: **Psalm 119:103, Mark 4:14, Hebrews 6:5, 1 Peter 2:2**

5. In what ways does God's Word sustain and nourish us just like food? See **Psalm 119:25, Luke 4:4; 1 Peter 2:2**

6. When was a time that God's Word sustained you in a difficult time?

7. In what ways does God's Word power our lives? See **John 17:17; Ephesians 1:13; Colossians 3:16; James 1:22-25**

8. Why is having faith in God's Word so important? **John 1:1, 14; Romans 10:17, Colossians 3:16**

9. "You are what you eat." Explain what this means. How could it also apply to making God's Word a part of our lives?

Bible Truth for this lesson:

God's Word nourishes us when we make it a part of our lives.

Acknowledgments

I am indebted to many people whose encouragement and support have helped me write this book. Some have also shared in the spiritual journey along the way. First in that category is the precious group of young women who made up that very first Bible study based on women of the Bible, where the seeds for this book were sown and began to sprout. Many thanks go to Lindsay McDavid, Mandy Sparks, and Kara Jenkins, the core of our little group. Together we began to listen to the voices of the women who speak to us from the pages of God's Word and to explore the depth and breadth of what they have to say to us today. I appreciate each of these young women who shared their hearts, their insights, and their lives with me for the months we studied God's Word together.

My deep gratitude also goes to the two wonderful women who have been my spiritual mentors and best of friends, Elaine Carson and Beth Everett. Both of them went to be with the Lord during the four years that I was writing this book. Their faith, their generous hearts, their lives of unselfishness—always putting other people first—exemplify the spirit of Blessed Is She. They are greatly missed.

In the same vein, I would like to thank my dearest and oldest friend, Kelly Kurz, a true kindred spirit and the sister I never had. For 40 years she has been a part of my life, and I'm hoping for 40 more!

Most of all, I owe so much to my mother, Joanne Ullman Huggins, who also went to be with the Lord while I was writing this book. All my life she and my father, Bill Huggins, have been a great source of encouragement, understanding, and support. Mom always listened and never judged, and always gave me unconditional love and acceptance. She read the earliest manuscript of the book, and of course found nothing wrong with it! That early copy is in her top dresser drawer to this very day.

Many thanks also to friend, fellow author, and prayer warrior Debby Koesy Alston, who read and edited multiple manuscripts of the book, and wrote most of the prayers in the final version.

My special gratitude goes to my husband, Rick Jones, always and forever the love of my life and my greatest support.

About the Author

Elizabeth McDavid Jones is the author of nine books and many magazine and serial stories for young people. Her books have sold over 750,000 copies. Five of her titles are slated for e-publication in Fall 2014, as part of Open Road's new series, Mysteries through History. Elizabeth has won the Edgar Alan Poe Award and other recognition for her work.

Elizabeth is a lifelong member of the Methodist Church, and has been involved in both children's and adult ministries for many years. She is also a ten-year-plus veteran of Community Bible Study, an interdenominational, international Bible study organization with nearly 700 classes located throughout the United States, as well as classes in more than 70 countries and more than 40 languages around the globe.

A self-taught Bible scholar, Liz has an MA in Literature and teaches at a local college. She lives in North Carolina with her husband and children, where they share their home with a big brown dog and a mountain of dirty laundry.

CPSIA information can be obtained
at www.ICGtesting.com
Printed in the USA
BVHW070945190619
551408BV00004B/213/P